# Obscured

The Pursuit of Radical Self-Acceptance

---

Samuel Uriah Goodman

A Pale Horse Media Co. Book

www.palehorsemediaco.com

Obscured:  The Pursuit of Radical Self-Acceptance

ISBN 9798678730947

Published by Pale Horse Media Co.

9780578731711

**Other Books by Sam Goodman**

"Safety Sucks! The BULL $H!* in the Safety
Profession They Don't Tell You About." 2020

## Dedication

This book is dedicated to the memory of Layne Goodman and Tim Goodman – you both are deeply missed. Thank you for being my brothers.

# A Warning…

This book contains explicit language, mature situations, accounts of homophobic slurs and actions, descriptions of depression, suicidal thoughts, and more. All these situations are described in graphic detail. If you are sensitive to, or effected by these themes, It is strongly recommend that you do not proceed.

# Introduction

"Quit being such a faggot!" I heard the manager mutter; it rolled from his tongue with ease. He was referring to another leader that had just arrived at the office with a "bitch coffee" as he referred to it. A coffee that was deemed not masculine enough for this particular workplace. You know the type – extra whip and caramel drizzled deliciousness. The precise opposite of the bland and stale office coffee presently reducing to sludge in the breakroom. "Don't bring that sissy coffee in this office" he said laughingly. Everyone nervously chuckled and then proceeded to go about their day; pretending that what they had just witnessed was not atrocious. I remember my immediate thoughts well: "WHAT... THE... FUCK."

You see, I am a gay man. That word is not one that I take lightly; especially when tossed around as an insult. I am not the most "obvious" of gay men, as if that matters. The queer identity has been so stereotyped

11

and distilled down that many of us are inadvertently excluded and not clearly visible to those around us. As with all members of the community, I do not fit into a neat and pretty little box that screams "gay." As many of us know, there is not "one way" to be gay. I am not "obvious," especially in a workplace that requires steel toed boots, a work shirt, and jeans. When first meeting coworkers outside of the working environment, most have the "oh, I get it now…" moment. I am not ranting (yet). I am actually ok with my outward identity – I am just happy being unapologetically me – this butch, masculine, jock, queen that I am. Look, I am an "out-n-proud" strong gay man, but it is usually not the first thing that comes up in conversation. I do not hide who I am at all, I learned that lesson the hard way – lessons that we will discuss in-depth in this book. But I try my best to not start my introductions with "Hello, I'm Sam and I am a homosexual." I just do not feel like this A.A. type of introduction is something that one should be required to do. The point is this, if that is what it takes to have someone not toss around words like "faggot," there is a much deeper problem. If I must wave a rainbow flag and scream "Here I am!" to avoid hearing degrading, homophobic, and sexist comments, we are not nearly as enlightened as we like to think. I am not one that most would describe a "sensitive," but my sentiment remains the same. What the fuck? This story simply demonstrates that a deeper problem does exist; a problem that contributed greatly to the length of time that I hid who I was. At this time, I was not formally "out" with this group of coworkers. The manager made the general assumption that he was dealing with a "straight" audience. He then took that assumption a step farther; assuming that because he was in a room filled with "straight" people that he could just drop the "f-bomb."

The word "faggot" is a word that ignites a fire within me; it makes my skin crawl. As much as I love seeing words reclaimed by groups that they are used against, this one still irks me even when used in a more positive fashion by the community. When I hear that word used in a derogatory manner, my blood pressure shoots through the roof and I involuntarily clench my fists. It probably stirs up the same or similar emotions within you. Gay, straight, or otherwise, that word often ignites anger in those that hear it used in a derogatory fashion. So, I had to do something! Right? I had to act; I could not allow this injustice to stand! I cornered the manager and I explained how hurtful that word is and how psychologically damaging that it can be. I went on to explain how that word leads to suicide and depression and just how harmful his comments really were. He was shocked, stuttering in his reply he said "I-I-I am so sorry!" "I d-d-did not know how hurtful it was. I really did not mean anything by it." We continued to have a deep and meaningful conversation on the importance of diversity and inclusion in the workplace; we talked for hours on LGBTQ+ issues. This awful negative event was turned into an amazing learning opportunity for us both. We high-fived, hugged it out, and it was an awesome day – the end!

So, what is the problem? I did not actually do anything. You heard me right; I did not do a thing. I panicked, I froze, and I simply ran away from the situation. I was scared and I did not know what to do. Fight or flight kicked in; flight was the obvious winner at the time. "But Sam, you are supposed to be this out and proud queer crusader! You are supposed to be fighting to make the world a better place! WTF?" you are probably thinking all of this and more. I don't blame you; I was thinking the exact same things at the time. I was scared and simply did not know what to do. I had lived much of my life hidden away; years of covering had left my soul entrenched with guilt and shame. Do I speak up and "out" myself? This employer was not the most open-minded, if I out myself will it damage my career? Will I get fired? If I say something will I be labeled as "that person?" Will I be othered? These situations usually only gain clarity with hindsight. I can look back now and think "you ass hole, you should have done something!" and I can say to the Sam of then, "what is the worst possible thing that could have happened?" But at the time, I did not have the security that I now have. I wasn't even all the way out; I had just started that process. I did not possess the self-confidence that I have gained over the years and my skin had not yet thickened. More importantly, I did not have the courage that I now have. But, all of that is ok. You do not gain those things over night. You see, courage is not something that you are born with. No one on this earth was born a courageous person. Developing courage is an intentional act and it takes time. We develop courage by the simple, yet scare you shitless, act of facing the things that we fear. At this time in my life I was not a courageous person, I was not a confident person, I was not an evangelist of betterment, I was not a crusader for LGBTQ+ inclusion, and I was not on a mission to make the world a better place. At this point in my life, I was a "green" safety professional just trying to forge a career and make a living. I had only one simple goal. My goal was to survive. To survive within my chosen profession, to survive within my chosen industry, for my relationships with my family and friends to survive, and to literally survive life.

I start here because it was a turning point in my life. It hit me like a ton of bricks; "what the hell am I doing?" I kept thinking. I had just spent much of my life hiding who I was – pretending to be something and someone that I was not. I had spent years fighting a battle of depression and living in turmoil with myself only to "come out," but not really. I had finally found myself. I had finally started to reconcile the guilt and shame that had been instilled into me by hate filled pastors and religious teachings. I had cleared my mind of all the homophobic and bigoted things I had heard throughout my youth. Against all odds, I had finally found myself on the path to self-acceptance. There I was, a strong and proud gay man – but not really. I was still hiding in plain sight and trying to blend in. I had survived an experience that many young queer persons do not. I had "made it" and there I was wasting it. "No more – never again." I thought to myself. I was done being a chameleon; from this moment forward, I was going to begin the journey towards being unapologetically me.

I share my story and experienced to hopefully create betterment; to make the world a better place. Ultimately, I hope that this inspires others to share their own stories and experiences with the world. Storytelling is absolutely vital to make things better. Through the telling of our stories we can create massive change within our groups of friends, our families, our communities, our workplaces, and the world!

I believe this through to my core: People should not have to live in fear of being themselves. People should not have to hide who they are in order to please anyone. People should not be forced to excise massive portions of their personal lives to be accepted by their communities. People should not be driven to the point of suicide because they cannot be their true selves at work or at home, or because the word "faggot" is somehow still in style. I made a promise to myself after this experience; a promise that I intend to keep. I will not sit on the sidelines – I will fight to make things better. I will demand better. I will stand up for better. I will scream and yell for better. I will demand better from our communities, from our leaders, from our employers, and everyone around me. I will remain visible and vigilant. I ask this of you as well; we share the responsibility to make things better. Betterment is a group exercise; together we can make the world a better place. Making the world a better place sounds like a pretty damn good goal to me.

# Genesis

So, who am I? If we have not formally met, I am Sam Goodman, I am a father, a significant other, and a friend - first and above all else. I'm also an author, a safety professional, organizational culture geek, an entrepreneur, and betterment evangelist. I am the host and producer of "Really Fucking Scary Stories" and "The HOP Nerd" podcasts. I am the founder of Pale Horse Media Co. and HOP University. I am also a proud and strong gay man. Although I have always been a gay man, I have not always been all that out or all that proud – I was quite the opposite for many years. But I am currently living my best life; being unapologetically me. I have an amazing partner (one that had better propose pretty soon) and an amazing daughter. I am blessed with a happy and amazing life. But for many years, that was not the case. I was deeply closeted and depressed. I was filled with guilt and shame that had been instilled in me by my upbringing and a religion that was forced upon me. I felt that I could not be "Me." My personal life would not allow it, my work life would not allow it, the world would not allow it. That description is a far cry from where I am now. Throughout this book, I will share my journey and my experiences with you. I will share with you my path towards self-acceptance. I will tell my story in a holistic fashion, focusing on many aspects of my life throughout the years. I will share with you my stories as the chaotic and messy experiences that they were. Our total experience is what leads to who we are and the path we must travel to find out exactly who that is. Remember, it is all intertwined. These imaginary lines that we draw between our work, personal lives, and everything else, is bull shit. We must stop pretending that we exist in these neatly separated little isolated worlds. We ultimately exist in one world: our world. So, let's dive into my world by rewinding it a bit. Well, by rewinding it a lot. Let's start this journey way back at the very beginning.

I was born into this world on November 28th, 1988 at 8:33 PM at City Hospital in Martinsburg, West Virginia. My birth was "interesting" to say the least. My mother was surrounded by my aunts, uncles, and grandparents; all excited to welcome me into existence.

I come from a pretty large family and seems most were present to show their love and support. My biological father was not in this crowd of onlookers as he and my mother didn't quite work out. They had gone their separate ways well before my now birthday. My "bio-dad" (as I refer to him now) and I had the opportunity to get to know one another a little later in life; he's a pretty great guy. He has an amazing family, a wife and my now discovered little brother. But that is not for this story. For now, we have a baby to deliver. Halfway through labor my heart abruptly stopped, prompting an emergency Cesarean section. The stories from those that we're there all sound pretty similar. "Everything was going seemingly fine; then suddenly things were not fine." One aunt once shared with me. "We were watching your heart rhythm on the monitor and then suddenly it just stopped!" she recounted. "Alarms started blaring and then your mother was swarmed with doctors and nurses. They kicked all of us out and rushed you both to the operating room" she continued on to say. "We were just left there to pray, cry, and hope you were ok" she said. My mother remembers me coming out "blue" as she has told me many times in the telling of this tale. She vividly remembers the doctors and nurses swiftly beginning their attempts to resuscitate me. After a few brief moments of resuscitation, what I am sure felt like hours to her, a gamut of tests, and some scary moments for my family; I finally made my way to my mother's arms. Other than being born "dead" for all extensive purposes, being born via emergency C-section, being resuscitated, and ultimately raised from the dead by a group of medical miracle workers, I was a pretty healthy little guy. Surprisingly and shortly after this early brush with death, we we're released from the hospital and set off into the world.

Martinsburg was just a brief stopover, a blip on the radar. I honestly don't believe that I have been back since the day I was born. I guess that I have never had a good reason. Upon being given my clean bill of health and being discharged from the hospital, we traveled south. The trip eventually brought us to the small town in which I would spend the next 20 years of my life; a small "speed-trap" town in the heart of rural Appalachia in Southwestern Virginia. We made this pilgrimage south because the majority of my family had settled in this region. My grandparents were originally from the region and had since returned after spending time across the United States. My Grandfather was in the Army and later joined the Air Force. This obviously resulted in them moving quite a bit. After years away, they eventually returned and settled near that small town I mentioned. A small town called Richlands, Virginia. Though they technically lived, and I was ultimately raised in, a small unincorporated area of Tazewell County outside of the Town of Richlands. The community was known as Pounding Mill. This was our

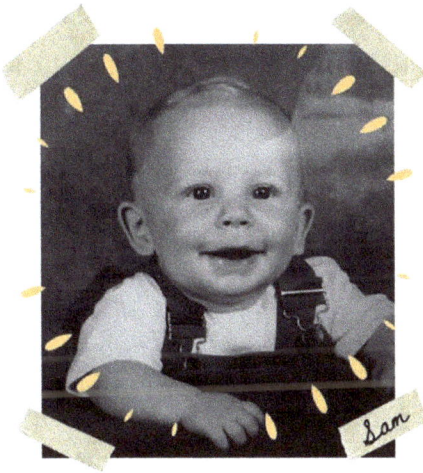

destination after leaving the hospital, my grandparents' house. This house would soon become my own; their home would soon be my home as well. Although there was some back and forth, my grandparents ended up becoming my parents. I have a good relationship with my biological mother. As I mentioned, I also have grown to know my biological father. Listen, times were tough, and shit happens. For whatever reason I was ultimately adopted by my grandparents; an adoption that I am so thankful for. They became my parents, the best parents anyone could ask for. So, let me help to eliminate any confusion right here and now. From this point forward when I refer to my mother, father, mom, dad, or the like – I am referring to Harold and Geneva Goodman. Biologically, they would be my maternal grandparents. But they are my one and only true set of parents.

Harold, my late father, later told me that he knew that they were going to adopt me that day that we arrived from the hospital. He always said, "I knew from the moment that they laid you in my lap – you were mine." Several years later his prediction was proven correct as I was legally adopted by them. I am thankful every day that I was raised by such amazing and great people. Though, my mother and I have had our share of differences, I was very fortunate. I would not change things for the world. We will dive into some of that struggle and some of those differences a little later; at this point I'm just a happy little kid. A blonde haired and blue-eyed little boy. I vividly remember asking them both shortly after my adoption what I was supposed to call them. I remember being jealous of other kids that would talk about their "mom" or their "dad." I would never quite know how to refer to them. I guess this is "being adopted struggles." Although in my heart, I knew that they were my parents, I still had a relationship with my biological mother. But to me, she was my birth mother – not my "mom." I was a confused little guy there for a moment, but they quickly helped alleviate my confusion. I just asked them outright one day "what should I call you all?" I'm sure that this question was just as confusing to them at the time as it was for me. I remember their response well, "whatever you are comfortable calling us." They continued, "we are your parents, but you call us whatever you are most comfortable with." I quickly landed on and blurted out "mom and dad!"

I have so many great memories from this time in my life. So many that it would honestly be hard to write them all down. Dad had recently retired from the mines, and mom had stayed home to raise me. I was an amazingly fortunate kid. I had a loving and caring set of parents; parents that showered me with love and attention. Parents that were present. Parents that really focused on teaching me and helping me grow. We lived in a quiet and quaint small town, one in which kids could roam freely without fear. Much of this portion of my childhood is filled with memories of spending time with my cousins during the summer months, being a "free-range" kid outside, going to church, and eventually going to school. Upon retiring, dad purchased an old Winnebago. We spent almost all of our free time traveling in that R.V. Upon going to school, I remember always being the kid with travel stories. When teachers would ask "Where did everyone go for summer vacation?"

My responses would always sound extreme and exotic to my 6-year-old peers; they'd sometimes even sound exotic to my small-town teachers. Maine seems almost imaginary to someone that has never been beyond a 100-mile radius of their hometown. Though we did not spend any time outside of the continental U.S., I had visited roughly half of the States by my tenth birthday. I loved traveling with my family and I still do. My parents instilled in me a love for travel; a love that I still deeply possess to this day. This is a love that my partner and I now share with our daughter. Travel was not just some leisurely activity or vacation. Travel for me was, and continues to be, an immersive mind-expanding experience. An opportunity to meet people and explore areas and cultures that I had previously not known. I do not know if this was my parent's intent at the time; to expand my perspectives and broaden my views. But travel had a profound and meaningful impact upon my life – an impact that continues to this day. There are a lot of amazing things about small town living. But one can also experience some deleterious effects from living the small-town life. One such negative side effect can be that one is never exposed to the beautiful and diverse nature of the world outside of that town. It is quite easy to "never come out of the hollow," resulting in an extremely narrow worldview. Travel can be such an amazing antidote to this dilemma. Travel was one of the greatest gifts that my parents gave to me.

I grew up in a very Christian household, southern Pentecostal to be exact. This seemed to be mostly my mother's doing. Pentecostalism was her chosen belief system. This means that it became our belief system as well. Though I never had the opportunity to speak deeply with my dad about his faith; the extremism of the Pentecostal denomination never seemed to fit his outwardly exposed values. I cannot speak for him because I simply do not know. But I do know that later in life, he and mom attended separate churches and I found myself eventually attending none. Much of my early childhood experiences are sprinkled with my mother's chosen religion. Most of my religious experiences during this season in my life were incredibly positive. I was not "different" yet; I was not yet unclean and secular! So, at this point in my life, I was well-loved and well treated by the church and its members. I was normal and godly! I fit inside of the neat box that the church had decided that I was supposed to fit into. I fit inside of the neat and clean box that my mother had decided that I needed to fit into. Oh, how that would all change in just a few short years. In an effort to further instill this faith, to limit my experiences with more "worldly" things like public school, and to pack me harder into that premade box, I was placed in a Christian academy.

I basically spent kindergarten through fifth grade attending a small Christian academy in a community known as Raven, Virginia. Raven is about a 20-minute commute from my childhood home in Pounding Mill. Nowadays, Raven is more known for its crystal meth problem than it is for having a private school. The school was tiny, so there were no buses or transportation services provided. I remember this commute well, because it was one of my more favorite parts of the experience. I got to spend time with my parents on the way to and from school, primarily with dad. We would have conversations and listen to the radio or some

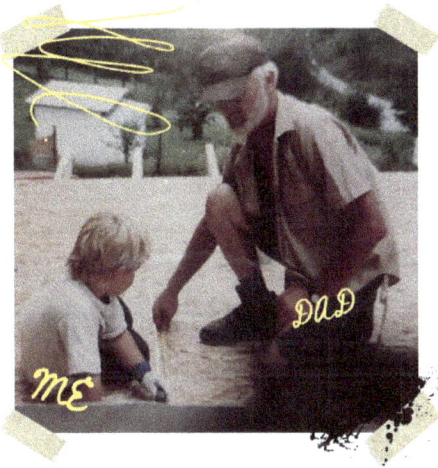

random cassette tape in dad's 1989 Extended-Cab Ford Ranger. My Christian school experience overall was not terrible. I honestly enjoyed my time there. I had some close acquaintances and a few really great teachers. My parents busted their asses to pay for private school tuition. While I may not be thankful for certain things that religion and this school tried to mislead me on, I am very thankful to my parents. I am also thankful to some of those really kind and wonderful teachers that I had; some went above and beyond to really teach us some core lessons around what is right, wrong, and more importantly, the in between. But, at the time I did not realize how insane this "school" actually was.

The only way that I know to describe this school now is as odd; looking back it was simply strange. The normal group experience of school was replaced with long stretches of silence and isolation. Classrooms were not really classrooms at all. There was not any actual teaching happening. These "classrooms" were all basically of the same design. There was a teacher's desk at the front of the room. Outlining the room were homemade cubes. These cubes were constructed of thick plywood and were built against the walls. They were layered with a thick coat of light baby blue paint. There were high wooden dividers placed between each student, and students faced towards the wall. Each workspace was equipped with a small paper organizer that held the student's workbooks, a pencil box, and a set of flags. The flag set obviously contained an American and Christian flag. In the center of the room was a "grading station" built to the height of the students that were occupying that class. This station was of an a-frame design; allowing several students to grade on both sides simultaneously. This was also homemade and constructed of thick plywood and had a thick coat of red paint applied. This grading station had red ink pens attached to it via chain and housed the answer keys to the workbooks that students were required to complete throughout the day. Students would basically face the wall and work in silence all day. Looking back, we were teaching ourselves via these workbooks. Working in silence was enforced to an extreme. The flags that I mentioned served a dual purpose; to force your focus on god and country, and to act as a signaling device. Students were not allowed to get up or verbally ask a question. Each of the before mentioned dividers had a small hole drilled in the top. If one needed help or to ask a question, you would place the Christian flag in your divider and wait for the teacher to come around. If you needed to take a leak, you would place the American flag on top of your divider and hope the teacher made it around in time.

I watched a close friend of mine nearly choke to death on a piece of hard candy one day. He began choking and was afraid to get up as that would be breaking the rules. Breaking the rules in this place meant a trip to the principal's office and a run in with the paddle. Oh yes, I said paddle. This place lived by the whole "spare the rod spoil the child" crock of shit. He placed his flag in his divider and waited; he waited until he just couldn't anymore. He finally stood up and made the motion that he was choking. The teacher grabbed him up in what looked like a bear hug at the time and applied the Heimlich maneuver. The round and white LifeSaver mint (ironic, I know) shot from his throat like a bullet and shattered against the adjacent wall. Her actions ultimately saved his life. I remember that no one really thanked her; everyone thanked god. I remember thinking "god didn't pick him up and save his life, she did! (She was one of the few really great teachers that I mentioned). Now that was an exciting day at Christian school, most were not of this caliber. Most days we would just work in silence, we would then grade ourselves in silence, we would then sit and wait in silence, and that was that. Maybe that is why I enjoyed the commutes so much; I was soaking up human contact and conversation prior to being depleted of it.

The school's curriculum was another problem entirely. We were basically our own educators. The school used workbooks known as PACEs. PACEs basically blended fairytale and reality into educational material; mixing bible stories with some basic educational requirements and selling it as fact. Also known as religious pseudoscience bull shit. I found out much later in life that many "teachers" at the academy were not in fact teachers at all. Many were simply facilitators. They we're not actually teaching us; they were simply handing us workbooks and babysitting. There was no teaching license required for that. By the fifth grade, my parents were beginning to take notice of the issues with the school and the lack of education I was receiving. They approached me one day asking about my happiness with school and asking if I would be interested in going to public school. As I recollect on many of these situations, my parents always seemed to consider my feelings on things. I told them the truth. I told them that I was ready to leave. By this point in my life, I was aware of kids going to "normal" school and I heard stories of their experiences. Surprisingly enough, many of these kids were from church. I envied their experiences and by fifth grade I was awakened to just how backwards my schooling was. It was decided, I would be going to public school the following year. In the public-school system of the county in which I was raised, there are a few different schools that you end up going to throughout your academic career. You would start with K-5th at an elementary school, you would then proceed to middle school for 6th through 8th grades, and then to high school for your final four years. Mom was uncomfortable starting me in middle school without any public-school experience. She decided to hold me back a year; I would repeat 5<sup>th</sup> grade in the public-school system. This was such a great choice on her part. I do not think anyone realized how behind I was educationally and socially from my time at the Christian academy.

A really funny story about starting public school; well It's funny now that I think back on it. A few days before I was slated to begin the fifth grade, I was approached by my mother. She set me down and said "listen, you are starting public school in the next few days. I think that it's time that we had a talk." I remember turning red and having a mini-panic attack. "Oh no! Oh no! Oh no! She's going to do it. She's going to try to give me the sex talk!" I instantly threw up in my mouth a little thinking about my mom talking to me about sex. At the age of 11, I obviously had zero grasp on what sex even was. But the thought of chatting with my mother about it did not sound very appealing. Though I did not quite understand what was happening to me, I was at that point in a young person's life where one begins to "notice" other people. I was already beginning to "see" those around me. More specifically,

I was "seeing" boys more so than girls. This deepened my panic. "What if she asks about girls?" I thought. "What am I supposed to say?" I remember thinking "I do not even know what I am feeling!" I had just spent my first 11 years of life hearing from her, and the church, that everything I was beginning to feel was wrong and would ultimately send me to hell. I was panicked and distraught on so many levels. So, there I was, braced for impact. I was going to get the dreaded "sex talk" and be outed before I even knew what "out" was. She said, "Sam, you have been in a Christian school for all of your life. On Monday you start public school." She continued on to say, "In your last school they taught you the word of god. They taught you the truth about things. They taught you the truth about creation – about how the world came to be." I remember thinking, "is this it? Is this the talk?" She said, "Now that you are going into public education, they will be telling you some lies. They will try to make you believe this thing called evolution." She proceeded to tell me how it was ok for me to "stand up and fight for god!" and how it was ok for me to tell the teachers that they were basically full of shit. I didn't quite realize the hilarity and insanity of this at the time; that hit me much later in life. I am at the point now in my life where it is more funny than anything else. At the time, I was just relieved that I was not going to have to talk about the "boys and the bees." My panic quickly faded away and I found myself starting public school a few days later. I was fully prepared with Christ on my side to battle teachers big and small on the evils of science!

My public-school experience turned out to be anything but this near satanic-panic experience that my mom had warned me about. It was actually pretty awesome; this year in particular was a huge year for me. Up until this point in my life I did not really have any close friends. I had my cousins that I would see during the summers and I had some kids at church that I would see on Sundays. Don't get me wrong, both were great. But my cousins were more like my siblings and my church friends were... church friends. The notion of having "real" friends excited me; people that I could choose rather than family or those that were chosen for me. I found some of that group during this fifth-grade year. On top of that, the educational experience in general was just vastly different; education was now enlightening. I was exposed to real art and science for the first time. For the first time in my life, my education was not administered through some clouded lens of religious pseudoscience. The bible was no longer used as a textbook! We were encouraged to pursue truth, we were prompted to be creative, and we were told to ask questions and to be inquisitive. All these things were demonized (pun fully intended) during my first years of education while attending that Christian Academy. Bible study was now replaced with art class, Chapel was replaced with gym, and hymns were replaced with real music classes.

A lot happened in the first 12 years or so of my life. I died, I was resurrected, and I was adopted. I was sent to the finest of Christian prison camps, and I traveled across the United States by R.V. I went from being a sheltered church kid with no friends, to a somewhat normal kid with friends. I got the ultimate Christian "sex" talk about evolution and I started to crush on boys. How much better (or worse) can this get? Well just wait, the hormones haven't even kicked in yet.

# Growing Up and In

I grew a lot during my fifth-grade year, well at least during my second go-around at it. I grew physically, emotionally, mentally, and even spiritually. I made huge steps in my young life; life was changing rapidly for me. This was an exciting and terrifying time. Even though just barely, I had started to "find me." This exercise in change had started me down the path of self-discovery; a path I was not permitted to venture just a short bit ago. I was starting to find out who I was. It was no longer about who my parents, or a church thought I should be. I still didn't quite know who "12-year-old Sam" was. But I would make even

bigger steps in the coming years to find out – some good and some not-so-great. I had just finished my first and last year of public elementary school. I was now on my way to middle school and I would soon be a sixth grader. I honestly had no clue what was instore for me. My young life was about to change dramatically once again.

It was a cool August morning; summers in Virginia always seemed to be beautiful and mild. The mornings and evenings would see massive downward temperature swings that would make being outside the preferred place to be. I was outside waiting on my bus to take me to school. My parents had driven me the first few days, we had also attended an orientation several days prior to my first day at the new school. During this session we had the opportunity to learn all about the school's bus routes. Now that I was in public school, the bus was an available means of transportation for me. In fact, the bus route went directly past our house. Though, I am pretty sure that my parents enjoyed this fact more than I did. I did not like riding the school bus; I was not a fan of its sights or its smells. I did not enjoy the slippery rock-hard dark brown vinyl seats, or many of the people that occupied them. The ride was always uncomfortable and too long; the other kids were loud and intimidating. It also required me to get up an hour earlier than if my parents drove me to school. This is the definition of a "nightmare" for a 12-year-old kid. It would also result in me being home an hour later than normal – home an hour later meant losing a precious hour of fun. Losing this hour put me one hour closer to bedtime; these were much simpler times in this young man's life. In order to make the bus, I would need to be outside by 6:45 AM. I remember vividly the dampness of these early mornings; the dew would still be on the ground. Hell, the dew would be on practically everything. I could hear the birds and squirrels rising with the sun; I could watch those going to work wave to me as they found their way to their cars. To this day, I can still close my eyes and almost be transported back to those moments waiting for that bus. I can see it coming around the hill, I can hear its low rumble, I can hear its creaks and moans as if it were about to rip itself apart. I can hear its brakes squeal as it slows, and I can hear the hiss of its airbrakes engage as the door would open for me to board.

Isn't it odd the things that we remember? The strange little snippets from our lives that make it into our "best of" reels. These seemingly meaningless bits and pieces that trigger something deep within our minds, deep within our souls. A smell that evokes a near instant flashback to another time, a vivid vision of a piece of a piece of life. Those small little things: these triggers assumed meaningless by most – they fling us down this path of remembrance. A feeling, a smell, a taste, a touch that resurrects a long-buried memory from deep within our cavernous minds. Suddenly and involuntarily we are thrust deep in thought reminiscing about a different time or remembering a person from long ago. We are near-instantly transported back; we find ourselves reliving a situation or an experience in our minds. The morning, with all its sights, sounds, and smells, reminds me of waiting for that bus. Upon hearing the birds come to life or feeling the dampness of the morning dew, I am there. I am near instantly transported back to those moments. I am 12-year-old me, standing by our old mailbox, waiting on that big yellow machine to carry me off into the world.

Even though I did not enjoy the daily journey itself, this bus was my gigantic yellow ship to freedom. It carried me to a land far away, a mystical and magical land that was full of friends, self-expression, and everything interesting to a 12-year-old me. This middle school, an institution that was feared by my mother, became my proving grounds. This is where I would discover many of the pieces that I would later stitch together to form my identity. An identity, that I have now grown to love. Much to my mother's dismay, this is where I begin to sample and try all that this world has to offer. I would find my likes and dislikes, life would begin to reveal itself to me, and I would begin to reveal some of myself to the world in return. I would discover my voice and I would unleash my inner rebellious nature upon this world, and upon my parents. I didn't quite realize it at this point, but these three years were significant; they dramatically shaped the person that I am now.

Sam Goodman

My sixth-grade experience was somewhat lackluster compared to the remainder of my middle school career. I was mostly just "sticking my toes in the water" and observing. I was taking mental notes on those that I thought were "cool" and those that I aspired to be like. I tried to stay out of the spotlight and mostly kept to myself. But something changed during that summer break; that time-off between sixth and seventh grades was almost magical. Over that summer, I built my cocoon and I transformed. It was a beautiful mixture of teen angst and hormones combining to create a new version of me. I discovered punk rock, I found skateboarding, and I expanded my group of friends. I traded in the oversized conservative clothes of my mom's choosing for ripped jeans and band t-shirts. I dyed my hair black, I started cutting off my sleeves, and pierced my own lip. I learned how to draw anarchy symbols, I smoked my first cigarette, and my first joint that summer. Long-gone was the quiet and shy boy of the year prior - he had been replaced. No, fuck that. He had been murdered; I killed him off! There was no longer room for him in this story. When I emerged from that summer ready for the new school year, I was a new me. There was no going back now.

As you can imagine, this new "me" placed that much more strain on my ailing relationship with my mother. We had vastly different world views; we were struggling to connect. We were opposites and were driving each other away in every way imaginable. As a rebellious and angsty teenager, if she was good then I wanted to be evil, if she was Christian then I wanted to be the anti-Christ, if she said "yes" then I would scream "no!" Hindsight brings with it huge doses of clarity; hindsight always seems to do that. At the time I thought I hated her. I thought I hated her because I thought she was ruining my life. Whether she admits it or not, I'm sure that she felt similar, if not the same. I was a teenage boy going through puberty; an obviously gay teenage boy now that I look back. I was confused, angry, and I was trying to figure out who I really was – I was trying to piece together who I wanted to be. Mom was an extremely conservative southern Christian woman. One that was, in her mind, battling the devil for my soul. The conversations that we would later have, revealed to me that she was also deep into her own struggles. We were both fighting a hard battle of self-discovery and trying to find out who we wanted to be. We were fighting to find out what we were to one another as well. I was torn between being myself or trying to please her. She was torn between being there for me or trying to please god. We had become sworn enemies; we were pitted in battle against one another. It was not by our choosing; it was just the nature of the situation. She would double-down on rules, control, pain, and punishment. I would retaliate by growing wilder and wilder. This cycle continued for years. She would scream "No!" and I would do it anyways. She would drag me to church, and I would paint my fingernails black. She would complain about the music I listened to and I would double the volume and would get a mohawk. We remained locked in this psychological war for years to come.

"You better not say a word to your mother!" my dad exclaimed as the clippers powered up with a loud "click." He continued, "She will be mad at you, but she'll divorce me." He said laughingly. We both chuckled, but we also knew that there was a healthy dose of truth in his statement. I could feel the cold unguarded blade press against my scalp; I could hear the clippers rhythmic pulsating grow deeper as it bogged down in my thick brown hair. My dad was giving me my first mohawk. Just a short while prior, he had walked in on a strategic planning session that I was conducting in my bedroom. A planning session that involved a complicated array of multiple mirrors, a steady hand, and a lot of luck. "What are you doing, boy?" he said. Dad had lovingly referred to me as "boy" for as long as I can remember. "Go under the kitchen sink and get a trash bag; I'll meet you in there in a few minutes. Oh, and get a chair out of the dining room!" There we were in my childhood kitchen, my head poking through a thick black trash bag and dad giving me the most rebellious of hairdos: the dreaded mohawk. He was damn proud of that haircut. His part in the "great mohawk conspiracy" of the Goodman household would remain a secret for the remainder of his life.

At this point, Dad and I had a much different relationship than the one mom and I shared. As I reflect on ways to describe my relationship with my father, only one word comes to mind: understanding. I do not harbor any vivid memories of my father demanding compliance with some command. I cannot recall a moment in which I felt judged by him. I do not have memories of him saying "You had better do what I say or else!" I'm not saying that it never occurred. Look, I am fairly sure that my father told me "no!" throughout my childhood. I am positive that he disciplined me, and I am certain that he judged me. My dad was a human; I look no further than my own faults as a father as proof. To what extent he did, I am honestly not sure. But I do know this, it did not occur at such a frequency that it was scorched in my mind. Dad approached things in a different manner; he seemed to give advice rather than make demands. He would give you the facts, he would sprinkle in some of his opinions, he would throw in some words of wisdom, and he would then leave it up to you to make a good choice. If your choices were not of the greatest caliber, he would let you feel the pain of those actions – at least momentarily. He would have that brief and silent moment of "I told you so;" that near-smile smirk that one involuntarily musters when proven right. He would usually then swoop in and save the day. As a parent, I look back with a greater understanding of his efforts and thought process. Dad's goal was not to forcefully prevent me from doing things that he did not approve of. Dad could see himself within me; he knew the approaches that would work and those that would not. He knew, from his own experiences as a young man, that demanding me to "do it now because I said so!" or saying "You had better never do X, Y, or Z!" would only result in me running in the total opposite direction of what he was asking. Dad was not telling me what decisions to make; dad was preparing me to make good decisions no matter the situation.

There is one thing that I can say for certain – my parents loved me, and I always knew how much they loved me. No matter how challenging any of us were, I knew the amount of love that was there. No matter how much more challenging things were to become, I would always know and feel their love. Mom and dad had two vastly different parenting styles; they were two vastly different people altogether. But I needed them both, and I needed them both equally. At the time, I could not appreciate this fact. I did not have it in myself at the time to truly appreciate them as the unique and beautiful people that they were. I was an asshole teenage boy with a chip on my shoulder, I did not have an ounce of understanding in me. But with each passing year, with every wrinkle that I earn and grey hair that I sprout, and with every second of passing time, I realize how much I needed them both. I realize the unique challenges and struggles that they faced, and I can begin to see my own hand in those struggles. It draws my mind closer to my own faults as a parent. They really balanced one another out to near perfection; I can see that now. Their relationship worked due to this balance, they worked as parents due to this balance, and it is ultimately this balance that made everything work. As challenging as these times were for all of us, I still look back on them fondly. I mostly just look back and laugh, laughing at my wacky hairstyles and cringe-worthy selfies on old social media accounts. I look back thankfully that my mom put me in my place; otherwise I would be covered in terrible tattoos, in jail, or worse. I look back thankfully on the teachings of my mother and father equally. But little did I know at this point that life was about to throw me a curveball. A curveball that would change the course of my life forever. A curveball that was known, but that would now be verified.

Sweat, grass, dirt, and cheap cologne; It was that musty teen-aged boy locker room smell. The smell of puberty and young men that had recently become conscious of their own bodies; they masked this self-consciousness with copious amounts of off-brand cologne. Welcome to grade-8 boys gym class, I'm Sam and I'll be your tour guide. We had just returned from the baseball field; this field spanned the distance between the middle school and high school. It was an expansive complex; you could see where the schoolboard invested its money. They really doubled down on their state championship level baseball and football teams. We had just spent much of this gym period running laps around those perfectly manicured fields and had just started the long walk back. I was itchy with the freshly cut grass stuck in my shoes. I was beaten down by the sun; It was a hot and humid Virginia day. "God, I hate gym class." I muttered under my breath. This was the epitome of hell on earth for a kid like me. "Why can't I just skateboard for gym?" or "They should let me do a double period of art instead of this stupid shit!" I would think to myself. The school never quite seemed to take my opinion to heart; no matter how many times I would carve "gym sucks!" into the thick blue, most certainly lead-based, paint of my gym locker.

We had just made it back from our long and grueling quest for physical fitness. There we were, squeezed together tightly in a single file line. We looked like ducklings following our mama duck. In this case, mama duck was a gym teacher in his late 50's who was wearing bright green tearaway sports pants, a tucked in stripped polo shirt, a whistle around his neck, and had a clipboard in hand. He was leading us safely back to where we had started this quest, the boy's locker room.

This was quite the precarious journey for twenty or so feisty young people. We had to cross the small, but busy, road that meandered its way around the school complex. From there, we would catch a sidewalk that would lead us past the gyms ticket booths and into a side door that went directly into the main gymnasium. We would then be required to navigate a narrow hallway and squeeze through a small single door that went into the locker room from beside the bleachers. This journey felt like it took days. I was in a rush; I wanted to grab my stuff and get changed before the locker room was flooded with stinky boys. I was one of those self-conscious and cologne-soaked boys myself; every young man is at some point. I had also experienced the cruelty of other teenage boys, as most of us had by this point in our lives.

When one is a little chubby and extra self-conscious, you learn a certain amount of "life-hacks" out of necessity. You learn a certain amount of "pro-tips" out of the sheer need for survival. This was one of mine. If I hurried in and got changed before everyone else, I could avoid the whole "locker room hazing" thing that everyone else seemed to find so fun. Finally, the line broke free and started to move; mama duck had given the ok to enter. I was in luck; I was towards the front! It looked like I was home free as I hurried around the L-shaped hall and made my way quickly towards my locker. Boom! I was stopped dead in my tracks by someone that was blocking my locker. "Oh god, who is this?" I thought to myself. I recognized him; my plan was not yet ruined. He was a friend of mine that I had made back in elementary school. His locker was directly above mine and somehow, he had beaten me in. I quickly breathed an audible sigh of relief. He turned around when he heard me. "Oh, hey man!" he said, and turned back towards his locker. He was tan, sweaty, and hadn't a shirt in sight. I could see the beads of sweat beginning to break and roll freely down his skin. Starting between his shoulder blades, they would slowly roll towards the small of his back, where they would come to rest. I had never noticed him before, at least not in whatever way this was. I did not realize how handsome he was until this moment. I never realized that men were handsome at all until this moment. He turned around and smiled, "do you need around me?" I momentarily froze. "Are you ok? Do you need some water? It was pretty hot out there. You look rough." Finally, I snapped out of it. "N-n-n no no no I'm ok!" I muttered. "I'm just, um, I need to, like yeah, talk later!" I blurted out. I abruptly turned around and powerwalked my way across and out of the locker room. I did not stop until I burst out into the hallway.

I could feel the cool air of the hallway envelop my damp gym shirt. It was like a cold and shameful hug from god himself. My mind was racing, "what the hell was that," I thought to myself. "Stupid, stupid, stupid," I kept repeating in my mind. This was it, I had "noticed" and there was no going back. No matter how deep I would try to push my feelings down, no matter how buried they would become, no matter how far I would take my cover, and no matter what I would try to do to change who I was – I now knew. I had a brief and momentary glimpse at every desire that would soon be boiling over within me. The realization of what had just happened hit me quickly; it hit me standing there in that cold filthy hallway. My tennis shoes squeaked loudly against the smooth tile floor as I walked back towards the locker room door. Tears began to roll down my cheeks and I thought "what now?" With a loud and siren-like buzz, gym was over. I quickly dried my eyes and fell in line with the masses heading towards their next class. I wore those smelly gym clothes for the remainder of that day. A pungent reminder of my earth-shattering realization; my shame on full display.

From that moment on, deep down, I knew that I was gay. However, it took me a long time to understand that there was nothing wrong with me. I grew up in a hellfire and brimstone church; I grew up with a hellfire and brimstone mother. On top of that, I grew up in a hellfire and brimstone town. All three preached that what I was feeling made me an abomination; something that was not even worthy of life in their eyes. My feelings for that handsome and nice young man were blasphemous and would "damn my soul to hell." As "punk" and rebellious as I had become (or at least thought that I was), I was still clinging to religion as a security blanket. I could not "turn my back on god;" this one singular "truth" that had been indoctrinated within me since birth. So eternal damnation was a very real, and very scary thing to me at that time. The thought of spending all of eternity in a "pit of hell" is a pretty heavy thought for a 14-year-old to face. An even worse thought than the risk to my eternal soul, was the fact that I would face complete and total social destruction. I had the opportunity to see firsthand the horrors that befell those that came out, they were quickly moved to the bottom of the small-town food chain. Kid's can be the cruelest of sorts. Those young people, the ones that I now realize were so much braver than I, suffered at the hands of those around them. I, along with my peers, had a front row seat to bear witness to their suffering. Kids can be cruel, but they were not alone. From teachers, preachers, parents, kids, and what seemed to be everyone, they would be ridiculed and made fun of. They would be treated poorly, or at the very least not the same or equal. They would be "othered," and there was no coming back. God and this small town had spoken – gay meant different and different meant bad. There was only one rule in this small-town hierarchy: don't be different – or else! I could not be gay! God said I should not be gay, small town society said that I should not be gay, everything that I had experienced and been taught in my 14 short years said that I should not be gay. So, I did what any good and god-fearing small-town kid would do. I wasn't gay. I did everything within my power to try to be the exact opposite of everything I thought it meant "to be gay," all the way down to the token girlfriend. A trend, that unfortunately, would not be short lived.

The school's buzzer erupted in a god-awful sound, just as it did every hour or so throughout the day. It sounded like we should take cover, rather than scurry from the halls and into our classrooms. The middle school was the most modern school in our county, the crown jewel of the school system. It featured such modern technology as digital buzzers, rather than the old-style bells of yesteryear. This screeching cousin of the alarm clock would make even the toughest person wince like nails on a chalkboard, but maybe that was the point. Either way, this sound meant one thing and one thing only, I was late. I made it through the door just before it was shut in my face; I made it by the skin of my teeth. "One more time Mr. Goodman, one more time!" My teacher shouted as she shut the door behind me. Ah, second period English. I rushed my way across the room, my feet thumping on the tattered grey carpet floor. This "modern" school of the future was more like a shabby old office building than anything else. From the flickering fluorescent lights overhead, to the pale grey carpeted floors, this place screamed D-U-L-L. The chosen color pallet of grey, light grey, dark grey, and faded grey, I am certain was chosen from the State Bureau of Prisons catalog. Nevertheless, I had made it. Today was a good day; it was Friday and I had avoided detention this week. I made my way into the center row, down seven seats, and there I was, home sweet home for the next 45-minutes of my life. The now primitive style television, one that was mounted in the front right corner of the room, sprang to life with a crackle. It's static and electrical buzz could mean only one thing; we were watching a movie! Happy Friday to me! The teacher briefly announced what we were to watch, dimmed the lights, and proceeded to bury herself into a book. I was 15 minutes into some literary classic, and I was fighting a hard battle to keep awake. My eyes would simply not remain open, no matter how hard I seemed to try. I was thinking, "you just avoided detention, let's not get it now." I was startled and quickly sprang wide-awake when a neat and non-descript folded piece of paper made its way onto my desk. I quickly grabbed it and pulled it under the desktop and out of sight. I fiddled with it trying to discover what it was. "To: Sam," I read aloud softly to myself. This is where it started, this is where I pushed farther and farther away from who I really was. This was a defining moment that led me down a long and painful path; a road that I would walk for years to come. I discovered a new "life-hack;" a new survival skill. I had an admirer, an admirer that would soon be my first girlfriend. I was no longer a confused and single kid; I was no longer living the bachelor life. I had a girlfriend and a girlfriend was the ultimate cover. A cover story and a dynamic that I would master over time. A story that would even begin to fool me. Though this relationship would only last a matter of weeks, years in the world of middle schoolers, I had now affirmed to the world just who I was. I had locked in my image; I was now "straight." I was not only straight, but I had joined the ranks of those who were dating. This was an exclusive club, and I was in it. I was not only straight, but I was now cool! Though this relationship was just a blip on the radar, there were many more to come. There were much grander and deeper lies around the corner; this was just the beginning.

"Pink is for girls you pussy!" I heard screamed loudly from across the gym. A small group of 8th graders were verbally attacking an underclassman that had dropped off a note from the principal's office. What was his crime, you might ask? He wore the wrong color of shirt to school that day and found himself in the wrong place at the wrong time. God what is it with teenage boys and gym class? It just never seems to end well. Another young man heard the commotion and blurted out "homo!" loudly from the other side of the gym; the class erupted with laughter. Even the gym teacher cracked a smile before interrupting, "boys, boys, if the fella likes pink, he likes pink." He said before asking them rather nicely to, "cut out the noise and knock it off." Everyone was high-fiving and laughing about how great of an experience they just had; like hunters returning with and celebrating a fresh kill. This testosterone fueled and cheap cologne-soaked pack of "great hunters" had scored a victory. They had taken down a 6th grader with just a few mere homophobic slurs. They had surrounded their prey, they had cornered him, and they had pounced. He didn't even stand a chance. I am not throwing these young men under the bus; I want to say that right now. They were not taught any better; we were not taught any better. The vast majority of these people grew up to be amazing and accepting adults. We lived, we learned, and we got better. Sure, some remained shit heads. Some always remain shit heads. But many became allies and some even came out.

"Oh fuck, oh fuck, oh fuck, here he comes" I thought to myself. It was my locker buddy, the boy that I had first "noticed," and the boy that I had just spent the last several months trying to avoid. I was instantly nervous and shaky; I could feel the cold sweat beginning to form on my body. I could feel my palms growing sweatier by the second, and I was near-instantly out of breath and overcome with this cold, prickly, and hot sensation. It felt as if I was going to melt into the shiny wooden floor beneath my feet. "Whoa, you don't look so great," were the first words out of his mouth; fucking Deja vu. "You must be really getting it at basketball today" he said. I stuttered trying to formulate a response but nothing meaningful would come out; god he was beautiful. "Did you see what just happened? Crazy, huh?!" This was it; he was going to become my knight in shining armor. He was going to go from being a guy that I "noticed" to a guy that I liked. I just knew that he was going to defend that kid. I was certain that he was going to show me that he held a rightful place as my first real crush. He was going to show me that there were decent and accepting people in my little small-town world. He was going to show me that I would have allies and be accepted. This was it! "What a fag! Right?" he said. My stomach dropped and I began melting into that shiny waxed basketball court. I stuttered and stumbled with my words; I pushed them up from deep within my gut. "Yeah, such a fag," I said while nervously laughing. He chuckled and trotted past me, joining the basketball game taking place behind me. "Yeah, such a fag," I thought, and that was that.

I managed to avoid him for the remainder of that school year. He ended up moving to another state over the summer. That was one of the last times I ever saw him. The last real words I remember my first crush saying to me, other than a random "hey bro!" was "What a fag! Right?" I don't blame him; this kid had a good heart. You know those people, the ones that you can just feel goodness radiating from within them, that was this kid. I'm certain that this "goodness" was a sizeable portion of what attracted me to him. I cannot blame him; he was fighting that same fight that we all were. We were fighting the battle of fitting in. We were fighting the battle of not being deemed as "different." He should have been taught better, we should have been taught better, I should have been taught better. I lost track of him after he moved, so I can't really say with any honesty what happened to him. I like to think that he turned out ok; I'm fairly certain that he did. Either way, he showed me a short-lived glimpse of who I was. Something, that to this day, I am still extremely thankful for. On the other hand, hearing those words, especially from him, drove me that much deeper undercover. I would spend the remainder of my 8th grade year pursuing and obtaining girlfriends, earning a reputation as a "ladies man" of all things, joining in with that pack of predatory hunters that were seeking and destroying "different," and ultimately suppressing my feelings so deeply that I myself lost track of who I was. I was a young, scared, and confused gay kid, and I had nowhere to turn.

This time in my life was so important in the long run, I can see that now as I look back. I learned a lot over these few years; they were brief but extremely meaningful to my life. I first discovered music and art; I found so many things that I still love to this day. I poured myself into creating music, and I started to find my own personal style. So much of who I am now, has roots in this season. I did a lot of "finding" over these three years. But somethings that I found; I quickly hid. Unfortunately, one thing that I became exceptionally good at during this time was hiding. I became a master of hiding those bits and pieces that were just too different for those around me to accept. I had started building an image to shield my true identity from the world, an image that would get better and more polished with each passing year. A mask that was so well constructed that no one could see me for who I was, or so I thought. This mask fooled most; I was just a normal straight kid. But no matter how hard I tried; I could never quite fool myself.

# The Highs and Lows of High School

"What up?" I heard tossed across the hallway towards me. "Hey man, same old!" I lobbed back as I maneuvered my way through a maze of people. A roll to the left, a juke to the right, full steam ahead and I was there. With a quick spin of the dial I entered 38-16-22, followed by a loving smack. I yanked up on the lever to open my locker; it opened. "Hell yes, first try!" I thought to myself. I grabbed a worn biology book, one that was being physically held together with several years' worth of duct tape. Seriously, you could date this book by cutting out a wedge and counting the layers of sticky and melting tape. Oh, have you seen the sports fields? They are immaculate. It really shows where the school board invests their money. I slammed the locker door shut and it emitted a loud metallic "clank." Off I went, back into that maze of people. Meet 17-year-old Sam, he's pretty cool if I do say so myself. A lot has happened over the last few years. Much has changed; much has remained the same.

High school started like middle school; I didn't really dive in headfirst. In the beginning it was more of a slow burn. It took me a bit to wrap my head around the entire situation; it took a couple years of growing up. But by the 11$^{th}$ grade, it was rapidly exploding as if it were doused in gasoline. I went from a shy kid with no friends to a loud kid with lots of friends swiftly; high school will do that to you. I honestly can't remember anyone that I was not at least friendly with. I had a close inner-circle of people that I spent much of my time with. But beyond my immediate friends, I seemed to be friends with most everyone. I had somewhat outgrown my emo-ish and punk wardrobe of middle school; now

opting for a more "preppie" look. Simply put, I was fitting in. I had now mastered the art (and deception) of not being different. I was not just fitting in; I was kind of popular. I would spend my weekends at high school football games, attending or throwing parties, hanging out with a gaggle of friends, and doing everything else that raucous high schoolers of that day would get up to. Things were going surprisingly well for the 17-year-old version of me.

I really need to say this; high school was fun. Honestly, high school was kind of a blast! I cannot paint you a picture of a sad, depressed, and closeted Sam. That picture would simply not be true; it would at least not be completely accurate. Yes, I was deep-deep-deep in the closet. I had suppressed my instincts so deeply that I had almost forgotten about them – almost. My urges were ever present; they would often creep into view of my mind's eye. While maintaining a slew of girlfriends, I was also head-over-heels in love with several guys. There was only one problem: none of the involved parties knew about it except for yours truly. I was living my "best life" in my head; just a fleeting homoerotic fantasy that I thought would surely pass. This fantasy and these feelings were easily suppressed, pushed down, and not allowed to see the light of day. I had mastered my image; I was great at keeping my secret. Even with this amount of suppression, high school was kind of a great time in my life. I look back on it fondly with many great memories. Even though I was hiding a significant portion of myself; hope remained. Hope that one day I would escape this backwoods town, that I could be true to myself, and that I could show that self to the world. I was a hopeful and happy kid, I was not picked on or bullied, I had great friends that I made amazing memories with, I grew closer to mom and dad, and we all shared a pretty great relationship during this time. In high school life was good, life was simple, life was fun, and all I needed to do was maintain. Maintain this image that I had so masterfully crafted, and just keep my head down. I just needed to maintain my secret. But as they say, "A secret is only a secret as long as only one person knows it." Life was about to get just a little more complicated.

I felt a strong "bzzzzz, bzzzzz, bzzz," in my pocket; my buzzing phone was seeking to gain my attention. As quickly as the first round concluded, there was another barrage of muffled buzzes. I again ignored; I was in class. I was not only in class, but this teacher was a notorious phone-grabber. This teacher also had the reputation of being a "text reader;" extending the tradition of reading notes to the entire class on to this more modern means of communication. I could not take the risk of him knowing that I snuck in such contraband to his sacred arena of education. I could care less about the possibility of detention; I could not lose my phone! Cell phones were still relatively new; I had just gotten one the year prior. This cell phone had become a lifeline to my social life. Through this hinged piece of metal and glass, were my friends; this was the tool that connected me to everything. Losing it would be a fate worse than death; a fate worse than death for more reasons than one. Beyond being a connector to my high school social life, this device connected me to another world. A world that I had recently discovered through the internet, a world of other gay people. I did not date or hook up; I would talk to them. No really, I promise! I would meet someone on the internet, we would exchange numbers, and we would text. I had found out that I wasn't alone in the world! This would go on for a few days until I would have flash backs to "a pit of hellfire," the thoughts of "turning my back on god," the idea of my friends or family finding out, or it would get to the point of possibly meeting up. Whatever the

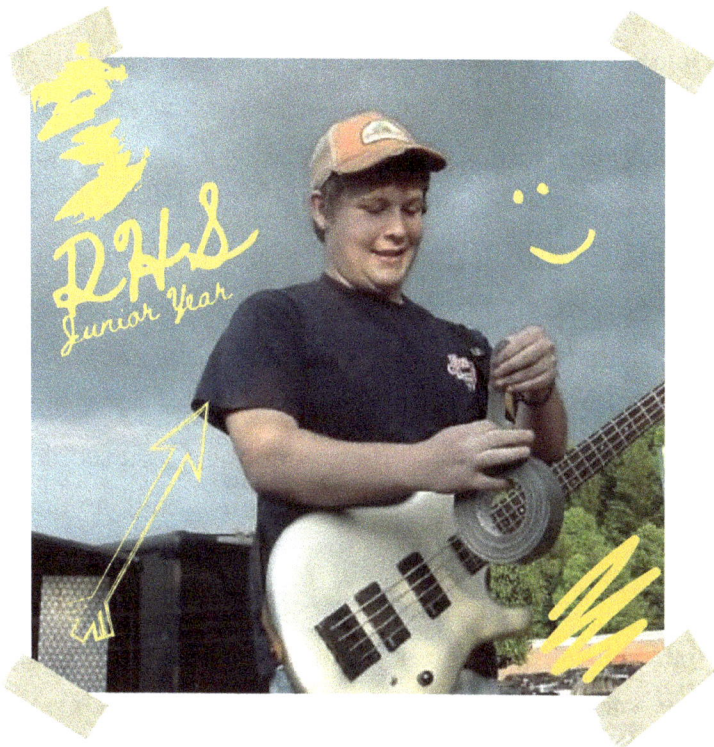

reason, I would quickly block and delete the number and pretend that it never happened. This cycle would go on for years, occurring every month or so. Now, I look back and laugh at just how ridiculous it all was. But at the time it all seemed so serious, life and death kind of serious.

"Bzzzzzz, bzzzz, bzzzz," once again – only this time the phones muffled vibration was magnified against the shiny metallic pole of the old-style school desk. It sounded like someone was trying to start a chainsaw, and unfortunately that someone was me. The teacher snapped to attention with bloodhound like intent; bound and determined to find the culprit. My heart was racing, my face turned flush, and my stomach screamed with discomfort. "If he gets my phone then he will look through it," I thought to myself as I rubbed my sweaty palms together. "If he looks through my phone then my life will be over," I remember thinking. You see, I had recently resumed my cycle of meeting someone on the internet, exchanging numbers, texting, panicking, deleting, blocking, and repeating. I was mid conversation with another closeted guy around my age from a few towns away. I had been talking to this guy for more than a minute; we were almost to the point of revealing our identities to each other. This was the farthest things had ever gotten. I had never thought of telling someone who I really was. I really enjoyed texting him, we were in a similar situation and had similar upbringings. So, I had not yet panicked and deleted this latest conversation. This conversation was on full display, unedited, and in its full glory on my phone. He zeroed in; he was coming right towards me. "Fuck, fuck, fuck, god damnit, fuck," I muttered under my breath as his shined penny-loafers made a light "clicking" noise against the floor as he rounded the desks. "This is it, I'm fucked," I thought as I braced for impact. The clicking of his shoes against the polished white and color speckled tiles rapidly increased. He was coming down my row; my mind exploded in rapid thought. "What will I tell my family, what will I tell my friends, what will I tell everyone?" I grimaced as I prepared for my fate; I could now only hope for a fast and clean end. "Click, click, click, click," he rushed past me and moved swiftly towards an open window at the back of the room. He fought with this antique chunk of glass and steel momentarily, finally managing to get it shut. "I don't know why they insist on doing landscaping in the middle of the school day," he said with a frustrated look. "It's so loud that we can't even concentrate!" he said. Luck, it seems was on my side today. How lucky I was, I did not yet know.

With a loud "ring," the old-style bells erupted with their metallic tones, signaling the end of the school day. The high school was of a much more traditional design, being built at some point in the mid-1950's. If the middle school was the crown jewel of this educational fleet, the high school was its disgrace. Though, I quite enjoyed its asbestos laden charm. There was something about that "old school" school that was just neat, all the way down to its cold war era bomb shelter and those traditional school bells. As the bells continued their long ring, I rushed and pushed my way out of class. I could finally see what all the commotion was about; "what could be so damn important?" I thought. I could finally examine what had nearly cost me my life. I rushed over to my locker, 38-16-22 followed by a loving smack, I yanked up on the lever to open my locker, and much to my surprise it again opened on my first attempt. "What is with my luck today?" I thought. I pulled my phone from my pocket and partially placed my upper body into the locker. This was a pretty common sight; the ole' "high school phone booth." The first message was from a number that I did not recognize. I opened it: "PARTY TONIGHT AT MY PLACE!!!!!!!" it read. Directly below it stated, "9:00 PM until whenever." The next in queue was from my best friend. She asked, "Hey, did you hear about the party?" followed with, "WE ARE GOING!" in all caps. The remainder of the messages were from friends; all forwarding on the invite and demanding that we go. All except for one; that boy from a few towns over. I fidgeted momentarily and finally opened his text. "Hey, how are you? I've been thinking a lot about our conversation and would really like to meet you." My stomach sank; those same feelings from the classroom were back. Those feelings that I had experienced only moments before, were now erupting from within me once again. My heart raced and my face flushed; my mind was on fire with fear and excitement. "This is it; I can do this. I can go meet him. I need to do this," I said to myself. A rapid "bzzzz" hit my hand like a bolt of lightning. I instantly snapped out of my deep thought and was thrown back to reality. He had text again: "Let's meet at the Bristol Mall tonight at 6:00 PM? We could catch a movie and get food?" he suggested. Bristol wasn't far; it was about halfway for each of us. I snapped back into thought, planning my night, and already inventing a cover story. "If I get ready and leave home by 4:30 PM then I will make it to Bristol around 5:45 PM" I thought. "That gives me until 10:30 PM, 11:00 PM at the latest, to make it back before midnight." Being under 18-years-old at the time, meant that midnight was the latest I could drive. If I did not make it home by then, I would face a fate with my parents that was much more dire than being turned into a pumpkin by the State of Virginia. "I can tell mom that I'm going with friends to see a movie, and I can tell my friends that I'm just not up for the party." I had it all planned out; It was down to pulling the trigger. "Mr. Goodman! Phone!" I heard viciously shouted from across the hall. "You're lucky I'm on my way out!" the principle shouted laughingly. "Get out of here and have a great weekend!" she said. Boom! I was right back to reality. "I can't do this! I can't do this! I just can't do this!" I said to myself under my breath

I had panicked and "fight or flight" was once again introducing itself to me. I stared at his text, and for a moment I slipped back into thought. My mind briefly connected with an image; an image of a sweet boy that just wanted to go on a date with another sweet boy. That image was everything that I wanted and everything that I feared. That brief and fleeting thought was everything in the world that I desired and could not have. The burden of who I was supposed to be would not allow this image to become reality. The mask that I was wearing, the one that I had so meticulously constructed, would not come off so easily. I stared at his text for a few final moments, I thought about that image, and then deleted the conversation. I blocked his number and the vicious cycle continued. But this time was different because this time it hurt. I cried in my car all the way home, ugly crying and blasting horrible emo music. Ah, high school heartbreak at its finest. This was my first heartbreak; my first real heartbreak was self-inflicted. As I pulled into the driveway, I spotted my dad outside doing yard work. I quickly dried my eyes with the inside of my shirt. I grabbed my phone as to look busy so I could keep him at bay; I could not have him asking questions. As I stared at the list of messages where his had just been, "WE ARE GOING!" caught my eye. "Fuck, the party!" I said out loud. I quickly opened the message and formulated a witty reply. "Duh, I'm in bro!" I finally text back to her. I immediately followed this up with "meet me at my place at 8:00 PM and we'll go from there?" and "will you text everyone else and see who's going?" My phone was once again erupting in a bombardment of buzzing; each "Bzzzzz" signaling support for the plan, or someone that planned on attending. I text her again "I'm ready to get fucked up, I need this, : / blahhhh" and I really meant it. This day was absolutely fucked, and I was ready to stoop to its level. "What a lucky day…" I thought to myself as I set in the car reflecting on what had transpired. My phone emitted a final short "Bzzzz." I glanced down at her reply: "Fuck 8, I'm coming now. I have vodka : ) PREGAME!!!!!!!" I put on my game face, I pulled myself from my car, and I made my way towards the house. I needed to get ready for this party; it was time to party!

You have certain people that show up at the right times in your life; they show up for a reason. With some predetermined cosmic mixture of timing and luck, you find each other. You can close your eyes and think of that one person that had your back, that person that pulled you through a rough patch, or that person that you could always confide in. These special people, that at particular moments in your existence, knew you better than you knew yourself. People that would do anything and everything to help you in any way imaginable; people that you would do the exact same for. You can close your eyes and you can see their faces; they changed your life. In high school, this girl was one of those people. She was my "person;" she could see through all my bull shit. She knew when I hurt, she knew when I was depressed, she knew when I was scared, she knew when I was happy, she knew when I was sad, she knew when I was joking, and she knew when I needed her to show up at my house with a fifth of vodka. There are certain people that you meet in your life, that change the course of your life, forever.

From the shower I could hear a light "Peck, peck, peck," on the kitchen door. "How the hell did she get here so fast" I recall thinking to myself followed rapidly with "Fuck, the vodka!" I sprang from the shower, wrapped myself in a towel, and rushed half-naked through the kitchen to answer the door. "What up ho!" she said as I whipped open the door. "You realize that you can see the bottle hanging out of your bag, right?" I replied. She shrugged with indifference. I let out an audible sigh and said, "Go to my room and please don't let my parents see it." I slipped and slid my way back towards the shower, trying not to fall or lose my towel. I washed the remaining shampoo from my hair, brushed my teeth, and made my way to my room. By this point, she had already retrieved two exceptionally large icey and syrup infused slushie drinks from her car. She was in the process of dividing the bottle of vodka between them as I walked in. "Don't worry I'm pouring yours heavy. It sounded like you had a rough day. Plus, I'm driving us to this party." She immediately followed this up by shouting, "yuck dude, ditch the towel for some clothes. You're like my brother." I laughed and grabbed the bottle from her hand, taking a large drink. "Fuck you!" I blurted out laughingly as I handed her the bottle and walked towards my closet. "Do you want to talk about it?" she said, as I started to look for something to wear. I paused for a moment; deep down I really did want to talk. I never quite figured it out, but it was like she could read my mind. "I know you," she said, "you can tell me anything." We locked eyes for a quick moment, and she repeated herself a little louder, "I know you. Please talk to me. If not now, promise me that you will talk to me before the end of tonight." I smiled and said, "I promise to talk to you if you help me find something to wear that will make me look less hideous tonight." She quickly snapped back with, "deal!"

"What the hell do you have me wearing" I blurted out. My plaid button-down shirt felt slippery against the freshly shined leather of her car seat. "Shut up! You look irresistible, you are so cute!" I replied, "I don't feel cute! Did you really have to pick out the tightest jeans that I own?" She laughed, "Yes I did! I did because your butt looks amazing in them. Do you not want your butt to look amazing? Would you rather wear those ugly cargo shorts and flipflops for the rest of your life?" We both erupted in laughter, snorting, and cackling for a few continued moments. Welcome to our pregame; a small and intimate affair just prior to the raging house party we were about to attend. We were sitting in her car, talking, drinking, and listening to music. We had driven down the road a bit and found a secluded place to park; that was a pretty easy thing to do in our little rural mountain town. We had to take this event on the road; we could only hide our boozing for so long under moms' watchful eye. Our laughter and loud conversation would be a dead giveaway. The night felt near perfect and it seemed destined to only get better. This was in obvious and stark contrast to the earlier half of the day. The night was beautiful; the cool Virginia air rolling through the cars open windows. The night air was bringing with it scents of the surrounding foliage and blooming wildflowers. The cool night air was churning and mixing these scents with the smells of a freshly cleaned car, perfume, and a slight tinge of vodka slushie. *A Perfect Sonnet* was playing across the car's stereo in the background; for a small and brief moment in my life I was at complete and total peace.

Her words sliced through my perfect night like a razorblade, "You promised" she said. I froze and I panicked; that cold prickly sweaty feeling instantly hit me yet again. I felt that deep and instinctual urge of fight or flight building in my gut. "What do I say to her?" I thought as my mind started to race. "Fuck! What am I supposed to say? That I'm gay? That I am not sure what I am? That I wanted to go on a date with a guy and I was too scared?" she could see my level of distress as I thought about how to respond. My mind was again on fire as I tried to formulate a plan to maintain my unbroken cover. "What am I supposed to do?" I thought. "Tell her that I'm not only gay, but that I am such a fucking coward that I couldn't even meet this guy?" "Say something" she exclaimed. "What do you want me to say?" I blurted out nervously. She set up in her seat, turning around to face me. Grabbing my arm and looking me in the eyes she said firmly: "the truth." She continued on, "I love you, you are my best friend, and I need to know what's going on. I am worried about you." My hands were shaking, and I started to cry. I could feel the cool night air brushing against my tear-soaked cheeks. While she was still grasping my arm firmly, she looked at me and said, "I've got you." That did it, after all her begging and pleading, those three simple words did the trick. After years and years of sharing my secret with no one, those words changed everything. They worked because I knew that she meant it. "I've got you," meant that no matter what it is, I'm here and I am not going anywhere. "I've got you," meant that it would be us against the world if need be. I did exactly what she asked me to do, I told her the truth. I told her everything; I came out to her. I opened the flood gates and I poured out my soul in that car on that cool Virginia night. After what felt like hours of me talking, she interrupted. "I love you and I told you, I know you," she said smiling. "I've got you," she said once more. She continued, "I love you but let's get the fuck out of here and get to that party bro!" The car once again erupted in raucous laughter. That feeling was back! No, not the cold, prickly, hot, sweaty, and nauseous feeling. It was peace; I was at peace. Once again, for just a small moment in my young life, I was at complete and total peace.

"Bzzzz – bzzzzzzzz" once again, only this time it was not coming from my pocket. The screaming culprit was coming from a bright, pink, and blue, floral covered bag that was nestled neatly between my feet. "See who that is," she said while motioning towards the bag. We were already on the road, making our way towards the festivities. I maneuvered my hands around the mostly empty bottle of vodka, loose money, and clothes; making a special point to avoid the more intimate bits contained within. "How many clothes did you bring?" I said laughingly. "That's a lot to only be crashing for a couple hours," I continued. This was a common practice for us; this was a normal weekend occurrence. Someone would have a party, we'd all attend, the party would roar into the early morning hours, and everyone would end up staying the night. We would find ourselves sleeping for a few brief hours to sober up, and then we would make our ways back home. People would be sleeping on the floors, in their cars, and some more prepared partygoers would even arrive with tents and sleeping bags. "Whatever!" she screeched. "You never know what the night will bring." Little did I know how much truth was in her statement. A lot can happen on a small-town Friday night; some good and some bad. Sometimes you'll find love, sometimes you'll find fun, and sometimes you'll find trouble. In my case, tonight I would find all three.

"It says to park in the grocery store parking lot and then walk up to the house," I read aloud after retrieving her phone from the bag. The car bounced with her rapid braking; the tires squeaked as she pulled a U-turn. We had just passed the towns small grocery store only moments before. My plaid shirt and tight pants slid across her shined leather seats once again as she made a hard-right into the parking lot, speeding across the lot and into a parking space. I glanced at the time on the cars dash; its small red identifiers indicated 10:30 PM. We were running late, coming out takes a few minutes, I guess. We quickly drank the miniscule amount of vodka remaining in the bottle; it went down with a distinct and sharp burn. We grabbed the few items we needed and locked the car with a "click" followed with a loud "honk-honk." "Phone, gum, wallet, and cigarettes. Check!" I thought to myself as we started making our way towards the party. I retrieved a piece of gum from my pocket; its harsh warm burn negated the lingering flavor of cheap vodka. I was buzzed, I was happy, and I was ready to party. "What the hell, give me a piece too, ass hole!" she shouted at me. I quickly complied, digging for the pack in my tight pockets. "Are you ready for tonight?" she said. I immediately snapped back, "Fuck yes!" She laughed and said, "You know what I mean, it's been a pretty long day for you." She continued, "just hang close, ok?" I begrudgingly agreed with a smirk. "Plus, I can be your wingman now! Let's go find you some boys!" she exclaimed.

As we made our way up the block, you could hear a mixture of commotion and thumping music. You could smell the pungent odor of bonfire mixing with the cool night air, the teenage voices echoed from behind the house. We made our way towards the side gate; the latch audibly snapped, and the gate swung open with a loud creak. Bottles clanked and the music grew louder, we followed the sounds of a successful party. We made our way through the damp dew-covered grass; the moisture turning my light brown *Sperry's* a darker shade of brown. The cool air and dew-covered grass invoked memories of a simpler time; memories of waiting for that school bus on those early mornings of middle school. But I did not have time for such nostalgia, we had arrived.

The night carried on like many of these nights do. We filled the night with drinking, dancing, loud music, and even louder conversations. There is no other way to put it, we were drunk. By 1:00 AM or so, the party had started to clear out. Those that were sober enough to drive, and those that needed rides home, had begun their symbiotic relations; knowing the roles would potentially be reversed the next time. Lovers had made their ways to cars and bedrooms to do what lovers do;

all that remained were the lonely few. Those that were single, those that were not seeking love, and those that were entirely too drunk to care. In my case, it was a mixture of all three. There were 9 or 10 of us that remained around the dying fire; I set there on a small cheap camp-chair with my head laid on my best friends' shoulder. We were both slowly finishing what remained of whatever cheap beer filled an old faded-red cooler that set next to us. The music had slowly faded over the night; the loud music and dancing had been replaced with small pockets of intimate conversation. As I glanced around the fire, I could make out the familiar glowing red faces. These were other small groups of friends that we would normally hangout with, mostly at events like this one. I reached towards my back pocket to find the box of cigarettes that I had so dutifully remembered to bring. As I pulled that light-green and white box into the firelight, I quickly realized that it was empty. I was never much of a smoker; I'm still not. But I would regularly find myself chain-smoking while drinking. I was usually much more prepared than I was this night. The eyes from around the fire fixated on the now empty box. Feeling the pressure from the group and realizing that I had more in the car, I blurted out, "I have another box! I'll go grab them!" I then heard a deep voice from across the fire say, "I'll go with you, I need to get my phone charger out of my truck." I locked eyes with him; I immediately recognized him. He was a senior classman and from what I knew about him, a pretty cool guy. I always remember him being very nice and quiet; he was handsome as well. I felt a sharp elbow collide with my ribs; it sent what felt like an electrical shock through my body. I glanced at my best friend confused and she returned a look of encouragement, followed by a joking wink. I quickly returned a look of "whatever," mixed with a lot of "shut the fuck up." I pulled myself from the rickety camp chair, retrieving another cheap beer in the process. I made my way around the dim and dying fire, following him towards the side gate. It creaked again loudly, and he pushed his way through; I followed him towards the sidewalk. "Tonight, was a blast, huh?" he said. "Yeah, it really was," I replied followed with, "How does it feel? You will be graduating in a few months." In which he responded, "I don't really know how to feel." I thought to myself, "yeah, me either..." Our small talk continued as we navigated the empty sidewalks and desolate roads making our way towards that parking lot.

In the small-town ecosystem, everyone knows practically everyone. I had never really spent time hanging out with this guy, but I knew him, and he knew me. We had shared friends and would bump into each other, we would have random conversations at gatherings, and we would find ourselves appearing in the backgrounds of each other's photos on social media. This was small-town life. We knew everything about each other without really knowing each other; almost everything. As we made it farther from the house, the smells of bonfire and beer were quickly replaced with the sweet and masculine scent of his cologne. I drew a little closer to him as we continued walking. I glanced over to see his face illuminated by the moonlight, I liked this guy. Those feelings, those that I was all-too familiar with, quickly returned. That hot, cold, prickly, and breathtaking culprit, had again invaded my mind. Though present, now it was dulled by copious amounts of alcohol. I was riding a high; a high fueled by the empowerment of telling someone my secret and cheap vodka.

As we approached my friend's car, I let out a loud "fuck!" He responded, "what's wrong?" with a concerned look on his face. "I forgot her keys," I replied. He shrugged and smirked, laughing in his reply, "Well, I didn't forget mine" followed by, "we can come back, it's not that far of a walk." Admitting my defeat, I followed him towards his truck; it's dark-colored paint and oversized tires splattered with mud and its windows tinted dark. He inserted the key and unlocked the door with a loud "click." As he crawled into the cab, he said, "let's hang out here for a little bit so I can charge my phone." He crawled across the bench seat and popped open the passenger side door. As the door creaked open, he said, "hop in!" I made my way around the truck and towards the door; the cold and wet beer that I had retrieved for this journey was still in my hand. I pulled myself up and into the truck, opening the beer as I set down. "You're my hero!" he said referring to the beer. I handed it to him, and he took a long drink. He handed it back and I followed suit by doing the same. He inserted his keys and turned the ignition backwards, causing the dashboard and stereo to spring to life with color and noise. He quickly fiddled with the knobs to turnoff the exterior lights and to dim those inside; we did not need any attention from passersby. He lightly raised the volume on the stereo; just enough as to mute the outside world. We set there and continued to chat, "Are you all a thing, you and ummm…" he slowly said. I responded with speed "Oh god no! She's like my sister!" he replied with a slight stutter, "You two are just always t-t-together so I just didn't know the situation." For the next few minutes, we continued to talk, laugh, and finish the last of that cheap beer.

In this moment something changed; something broke loose inside of me. A fire was ignited, and I could not extinguish it. I couldn't take my eyes off him; I was clinging to every word he said. The mixture of alcohol, cool night air, frustration, and desire, mixed to form levels of courage and self-confidence that I had never experienced before. "I'm going to tell him I'm attracted to him," I thought, as my mind raced. My heart was beating through my chest; It felt as if it might explode. I was shaky and out of breath; he noticed that the atmosphere had changed. "Are you ok? You don't look so great," he said. "Fucking Déjà vu," I thought to myself laughing under my breath. He could feel my stare; he was reciprocating with brief glances. I noticed that he appeared to be just as distraught as I was. We were momentarily frozen in time; staring blankly at each other and scared out of our minds. The truck was completely silent as the most recent song had just come to an end. The night was completely silent; so silent that we could hear each other's heartbeats audibly pounding. The silence was broken as another song started to play. As it started, he pushed himself from the steering wheel across the seat and grabbed me. He kissed me; I kissed him back. I wrapped my arms around him and slid downward in the seat; that stupid slippery plaid shirt and those tight jeans aiding in the slide.

We spent the remainder of that morning in that pickup truck; eventually watching the sun begin to rise over that old grocery store. That feeling was back; that feeling of peace. Another small and fleeting moment of stillness in my chaotic mind. I was at peace and I was happy, even if only for a few moments. We laid there in that truck talking about life and the struggles that we shared; saying the things that we had never been allowed to verbalize to another. We were hopeful; we were going to hang out and see where this could go. We were going to try to live out that image of those two sweet boys that just wanted to be together. We were ready to try to be ourselves, even if only in secret and with one another. We had discovered each other, and we were going to try. Optimism and hope can do a lot for a young and distraught closeted man trying to find himself. It can bridge the gap between where he is and where he wants to go, even if only in his own mind for a few moments. As the sun was continuing to rise, I could see a small and short silhouette making its way through the parking lot. It was her; it was my best friend. I sprang to life grabbing my belongings and "fixing" myself as to look presentable. I paused for a moment, staring back into his eyes. I kissed him and he kissed me back, wrapping his arms tightly around me. We smiled at each other briefly before breaking our embrace. As I rolled out of the truck, he shouted "text me when you make it home!" I agreed with a smile and waved as I shut the door. I rushed towards the car, arriving just as the doors "clicked" unlocked. I poured myself into the car simultaneously blurting out, "are you ok to drive?" She replied, "Me? Where the hell have you been? What happened to staying close? Look at your hair! What the heck happened to you?" I watched her anger quickly turn to frustration which in turn became wide-eyed confusion. "Wait a second," she said. "Where were you?" she said inquisitively. I stared at her with a telling smirk; I couldn't hide my pride. "Wait!" she exclaimed. "Whose truck is that? What did you do? You never came back last night!" she shouted, peppering me with a barrage of questions. "You left with…" it hit her. That look of anger and frustration instantly turned to a look of clarity; a realization of what had occurred. "Oh my god! Really? I was joking! He's gay?" she squealed. "Tell me, tell me, tell me!" she continued. We talked all the way home and I told her everything; I once more poured out my heart and soul in that car. I would do so more times than I could count throughout the rest of my short high school years; if that car could only talk. I could now tell her everything; I could really tell her everything. After picking up some sports drinks and some greasy breakfast biscuits, I had made it home. My mom was not home, but dad was wandering around the house. I tried to sneak past him but was unsuccessful. "Boy, where have you been? Are you ok?" I replied, "I Just spent the night with some friend's dad. I'm good; I'm pretty great actually." I made my way to my room and crawled into the cool sheets. I opened my phone and sent a quick message: "I'm home, I miss you, thanks for last night." I laid in my bed nearing sleep and reflecting on the events of the last 24 hours. "What a lucky day…" I thought to myself as I finally succumbed to the night before.

On that small-town Friday night, I found love, I found fun, but I also found trouble. In the coming weeks I would be hit with rumors and accusations, all questioning what had really taken place that night. My best friend was not the only one that had noticed our absence; several of the remaining people at the party had noticed as well. They ultimately took what little information that they had to work with and started rumors. They took the single fact that we had left together and masterfully crafted some amazing stories; teenagers are the absolute worst. Just as bad, they were not entirely off base. I would hear things ranging from, "I heard those homos sucked faces all night" to, "Yeah, I heard that they have been secret fuck-buddies for years!" "Yeah, right! I wish!" I remember thinking at the time, but there was some truth in the gossip that they were spreading. This was dangerous; if these rumors were believed they could destroy my carefully crafted image. I look back now with the realization that only three people truly knew what took place. All the other noise was just fantasy; it was pure speculation and rumor. But at the time, it felt very dangerous, it felt dangerous to us both. The two hopeful and optimistic young men that had discovered themselves in that truck that night, were gone. The rumors and speculation had replaced their hope and optimism with fear and shame. What started as, "let's give this a shot," took a sharp turn in the opposite direction. We had discovered each other; not a small feat in a tiny mountain town before the advent of dating apps. We did not, we could not, realize just how lucky we were in that moment. The fear of the world discovering us for who we were vastly outweighed this unrecognized blessing. What should have been the first steps in coming out, now thrust me deeper into the closet than I had ever been before. The grand plans that he and I had made would never come to fruition; we near immediately cut things off. We couldn't be seen together, we couldn't get caught texting, or hanging out, what would people think? Can I just say that hindsight sucks? It's a painful situation to look back on, especially knowing that it could have been handled so differently.

I quickly moved on from this night and the few weeks of gossip that followed it. I patched and mended my perfect mask; I worked swiftly to restore any damage that had been inflicted upon my sacred image. After a few weeks of hiding and mending, I resumed my same destructive cycle of meeting someone on the internet, exchanging numbers, texting, panicking, deleting, blocking, and repeating. Within a month I had a new girlfriend; I had now outwardly reaffirmed my straightness to the world. The rumors had passed, the gossip had come to an end, and I was once again straight. That 24-hour period was one of the most meaningful and life changing that I had ever experienced. Out of my 148,920 hours of existence, those 24 hours changed everything. On that day, I had suffered heartbreak, I crawled deeper into the closet, and I would suffer deep depression and regret because of it. Those 24-hours also brought me amazing and needed things. They gave me someone to confide in; a best friend that now knew the real me. She kept my secret and was my "person" for the remainder of high school, helping me to navigate life and being my shoulder to cry on. Even though I deeply suppressed it, that night also showed me who I was and what I wanted. That night, in that old pickup truck, was my sexual revolution. I verified something that I already knew, but it changed my life forever.

The remainder of high school, much like that day, was chocked full of wild ups and downs. I experienced the highest of highs and the lowest of lows; surviving high school is no easy task. But I did survive, and I made a lot of great friends and memories in the process. As for my best friend, we grew older, I moved to the west coast, she stayed on the east coast, life happened, and we eventually grew apart. But I am thankful for our time together. That cute boy and I met again on my "senior week" graduation trip. "Senior Week" was a rite of passage in which freshly graduated seniors would get black-out drunk for a week in Myrtle Beach, South Carolina. He was there with some mutual friends; people that I had recently graduated with. We got to spend most of the week together making up for lost time. That week would be the last week that I would ever see him; it was also one of the last times that I would see my best friend and most of my inner circle of people.

These years of our youth flew by in the blink of an eye; time would show us no empathy. That's the problem with youth, it all seems so endless. In the moment, life and time seems limitless. In our youth, we take for granted these meaningful moments and amazing people. We simply can't comprehend that it will all be over in the blink of an eye; we cannot wrap our minds around how life changing these experiences and these people are. High school brought me heartbreak, it brought me fun, it brought amazing people into my life, it brought me brief moments of love and moments of sheer terror. In high school, I kissed my first boy, I came out for the first time, and I went right back in. No matter the fact that I left high school deep in the closet, I do not look back with regret. It's easy to contemplate how different life could have been; what would have changed if I would have come out? What would the endless possibilities have looked like? One can always look back on a situation and imagine doing things differently: hindsight's a mother fucker. My point is this, and I did not realize it at the time, everything happens for a reason. In the infinite magic and wisdom of the universe, god, or mother nature, things seem to happen when they are supposed to happen. The right people find you when they are supposed to, you come out to your best friend when you are supposed to, you follow a cute boy to his truck when you are supposed to, and you come out to the world when you are supposed to.

# The Floating

As the water swirled across it, the hot dark asphalt turned a bright shade of yellow. With each blast of water from the light-green hose, a mixture of pollen and soap made its way from my car to the ground. The foamy yellow mixture traced the topography of the driveway as it found its way towards the ditch. I was performing one of the most sacred rituals that any 19-year-old boy can perform; I was washing and detailing my car. I was preparing for yet another small-town weekend. I lightly toweled down the excessive water and made my way inside to cool off. I grabbed a cold bottle of water from the refrigerator, retrieved my sticker-covered laptop from my room, and poured my damp and sweaty self into a chair. "How the hell did I manage a D," I thought to myself as I scrolled through my most recent grades. My first few semesters of college were not going as planned. I found myself attending the local community college; enrolled in the Administration of Justice program. College and I just

couldn't seem to click; we weren't on the same wavelengths. I would go to class throughout the day, play music as much as I could, and I had a part time gig as a security guard in the evenings. I would scrape by in class during the week, work a few shifts on top of it, and drink most of the weekends away. You could regularly find me at a party or a few towns over on the lake.

My life was on pause; I was in limbo. I was in small-town purgatory. I was a failing college student with the beginnings of a drinking problem, I was a 19-year-old gay man with a girlfriend, and making matters worse, I was becoming well-acquainted with depression. As I stood up, I pinched the lid of the laptop shut. It's metal and sticker covered shell slid rapidly through my wax covered fingers, hitting the floor with a sharp thud. "Fucking great," I thought to myself as I examined it for any signs of obvious damage. Noting its apparent survival, I proceeded to tend to more important endeavors; I made my way back outside. As I resumed my ritualistic waxing, I could hear a muffled ringing from inside the house. I figured that it was my dad calling; he had taken a job working in power plants back when I was still in high school. Dad would mostly work during the spring and fall, traveling all over the country from job to job. He was currently in the sleepy little coastal town of Oak Island, North Carolina. I heard the ringing continue uninterrupted for a few moments before finally coming to an abrupt end. I refocused on my work; I was nearing completion of my sacred task, when a high-pitched howl pierced the light music being emitted from the car. The howl quickly turned into a loud-sobbing moan as I heard the front door swing open and collide with the wall. I can still feel that shriek; it gives me chills thinking about it. I had never heard such a sharp and guttural sound, and I have yet to hear anything that compares. It was a sound of pure anguish, it was a vocalization of profound sorrow, and an articulation of the greatest loss one can suffer. I stood there confused and trying to understand this sound; grasping at logic to make sense of what I was hearing. My mind could simply not construct an image of what could cause such emotion. Within a few short moments, whatever the time that it would take for my mother to traverse the pathway of brick and mortar between us, I would know its cause.

This driveway where I would once wait for the school bus, the same driveway that I once cried over a boy that I had never met, the same place that I skateboarded as a kid, was now the backdrop for discovering the news that my dad had died. A hot and numb feeling instantly poured over me; a dull pain enveloped me as I stared at my feet in disbelief. My heart pounded and I could not catch my breath; that visceral urge to run hijacked my mind. I threw myself into my half-waxed car and sped from that still damp driveway; the tires squealed with my rage. I drove as fast as I could possibly drive, tears pouring down my cheeks and into my lap. I poured all my anger and frustration into the accelerator, half-hoping to not return. I soon snapped out of my trance-like state when It hit me; no one knew. So, like a blonde-haired grim reaper, I went visiting family members door-to-door to spread the news of death. When my macabre task was finally finished, I returned home. But I would return to a home that would never quite be the same. The numb blur of those surrounding weeks has long since faded from my memory; my brain continuing to shield me from trauma that I do not wish to relive. The acute trauma would soon fade, though the lasting effects of this loss would be added to my growing heap of chronic ailments.

I was angry; this is not what was supposed to happen. This is not the way things were supposed to be. Over the last few years of his life, dad and I had grown extremely close. He was no longer just my father; he was my friend. Sure, I was angry that my dad had died. But I think I was angrier that I had lost a friend. Dad was my ally; he was always my ally. I know that he would have always been my ally, no matter what. To this day, I still feel shortchanged by the whole situation.

Look, I have processed it, and I have accepted it for what it is. But this whole, "time heals all wounds" thing is kind of bull shit. Somethings you just end up carrying with you; they are invisible scars on your soul. Sure, they will fade over time and they will become less noticeable. But, no matter how much time tries to wash them away, those scars and their memories will remain. My scar was this: I should have come out to my dad. I was supposed to come out to him; I wanted to come out to him. I wanted him to see me happy for once. I wanted him to see me, the real me, the unmasked me, the real person that I had hidden from him for all those years. But I never did, and that is a scar that my soul will bear forever.

"Ugh... What the fuck, man!" the blurry and undistinguished character shouted at us angrily; I motioned in an apologetic fashion after we nearly knocked him down. I had lost a full vodka tonic in the process; most of it finding its way down my legs. We were out, out on the town! A small group of friends and I were bar hopping the night away, a now common occurrence in our 21-year-old plus lives. While making our way towards the nearest bar to find a replacement double lime vodka and tonic; my phone screamed to life with a loud "bzzzz." I could see its bright light illuminating the sticky bar floor as it shined through the slight rips and tears of my then in-style jeans. I quickly retrieved it; hopeful that it was a response to a message I had sent earlier. A message to a guy that I had been texting over the week; a guy that lived in this town. Squinting, I eagerly tried to make sense of the moving letters on the brightly lit screen. "Where are you guys?!?!" I sounded out under my breath. The inquisitive message was from my latest girlfriend; she was our acting designated driver for the night. She had dutifully driven us to our nearest college town; the closest place in which young people could find the trouble they so often sought after. My eyes rolled with discontent and disappointment; she was not who I had hoped for. I pecked at the screen to formulate the best possible reply that my alcohol-soaked motor skills would permit me to construct. "Be done soon," was as good as it was going to get. Returning to the group with a new drink in hand, I proudly announced: "I bought us some time!" Everyone erupted in a loud cheer, and the party resumed with added intensity. "Be done soon," meant 2:00 AM – a full 3-hours after sending the original response.

On the outside, life was a giant party. From the outside looking in, my life appeared to be pretty amazing. I built it to appear that way; I had nearly mastered the skill of fabrication. I was surrounded by amazing friends and always found myself getting up to interesting and fun things. My life was filled with nights like this one; endless alcohol fueled endeavors. Weekend after weekend, this was a never-ending pursuit. I spent most nights chasing a feeling that I could never seem to find. That feeling that I had only had brief tastes of thus far in my life, those tiny moments of calm. Small and momentary slivers of carefree stillness. I could never find the peace that I so frequently sought after; it was always just out of reach. If I could not find the peace that I so longed for, then numb would have to do. I was meeting my small-town problems with small-town solutions. If I could not feel at peace, then I was going to numb myself to the point of feeling nothing at all. With all this practice, I got pretty good at feeling nothing, or so I thought. I would always push farther and farther; pursuing that which was just out of my grasp. My frustration would build, the shame and guilt of who I was would fester, and fear would eat away at my soul. I would seek the remedy for this at the bottom of a bottle of cheap vodka; never quite seeming to find it. But each quest would make the next that much harder, pushing my now beloved feeling of "numb," that much farther away.

With the bars beginning to close, the more responsible one in this group started the tedious task of herding drunks towards the exit. This is not an easy task in a dark and smoke-filled bar; convincing those to leave that would rather not. Every group of friends has that one person, that nurturing personality that takes it upon themselves to look out for everyone. With this person, a little help, and a lot of luck, we eventually found ourselves outside. We were poured into the streets with a hoard of other bargoers, all stumbling their way into the night. "Beep-Beep," echoed from a makeshift public parking lot across the street; it was her and she was signaling that it was time to go. Her discontent was clearly visible through the windshield; she was not happy. We staggered our way across the street and into the awaiting SUV, settling in for the long journey back to our small mountain town. We had to hurry; our night was far from over.

Another common occurrence in both my life, and anyone's life that experienced a small-town upbringing, is something known as the "field party." This was the next stop for this caravan of drunken fools. We would soon be surrounding a warm fire and trying our best to get black-out drunk, racing against the rising sun. This is a beloved small-town institution; a tradition that we kept alive and well. Slipping and sliding on the dewy

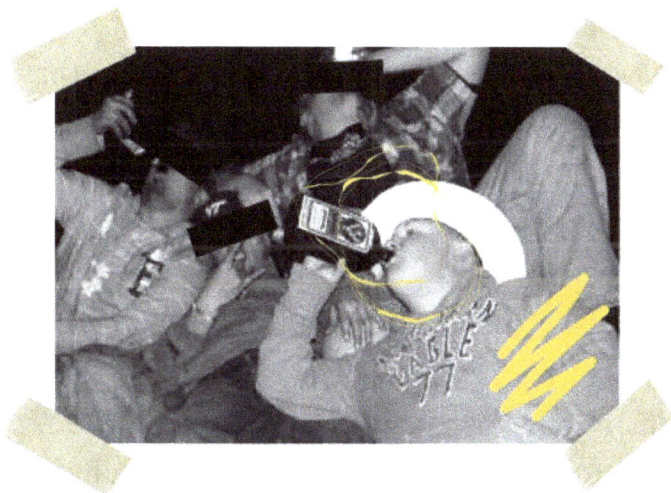

tall grass, the small SUV's frame creaked as it contorted itself to match the below landscape. We had just spent miles following a small county road out of civilization and into the darkness. The road had slowly slipped from beneath us, moving from asphalt, to gravel, and finally becoming mud. We had squeezed through a faded red gate; the accompanying cattleguard shook the car violently just before it released us into the tall green grass of the field. We followed the pale orange and red glow as if it were a guiding star; eventually finding its source. We had arrived and we were ready to resume where we had left off.

I continued my hunt for numb; spending the remainder of these early morning hours trying to deaden all internal sensation. I nearly succeeded, pushing my way closer and closer towards the edge of oblivion. Pushing myself nearer to feeling nothing at all; edging closer and closer to successfully killing off that portion of me. My plan was flawed; my plan had one particularly disastrous side effect. With enough to drink, my defenses would drop. My perfect mask would slip, my cover would fade, and my untarnished image would melt away to reveal the grim picture of who I had become. I was empty, a melancholy and depressed young man. I had become devoid of any previous hope or optimism; I was a person floating and lost. I had pushed so far away from who I was, that I could not find my way back. My mouth was watering; I was overcome with chills and cold sweat. That cold, prickly, hot, and panicked sensation poured over my body. It was swiftly interrupted by a loud, rumbling, and violent "Pffftttbrrrrrrrack," and a moist splattering that was muffled by the tall green grass beneath me. A friend rushed over to my aid, "are you ok, man?" he asked as he patted the small of my back. "I'm fine! Just leave me alone!" I angrily yelled out. "Jesus Christ bro, I'm just worried about you. What the fuck is your problem?" he fired back with confusion. "Me! It's me! It's fucking me! I am the god damn problem!" I quickly shouted back in my drunken stupor. "You have no clue; you don't know who I am. I am an awful person." I yelled at him. "What the hell is going on with you?" he exclaimed while shaking my shoulders; his touch near instantly snapping me out of my trancelike state. After a few tense moments the situation deescalated, and we found ourselves away from the group continuing our dialogue. "What is it?" he asked. "I can't really say; I can't tell you." I replied. "I'm just different," I said as I started to break down. "I just don't want to live like this anymore," I quickly spit out. "I can't do this!" I screamed in a voice as loud as I could muster. As I was sobbing, he wrapped his arm around me and offered me a beer. We set there drinking in silence. That is the last memory that I have from that night; I nearly found what

I was looking for. I almost found nothing, I almost found darkness, but not quite. Though I did manage to drink myself as close to the point of oblivion that I could.

I felt the cool dampness of my sweat soaking into the bed and surrounding blankets. My errors from the night prior were slowly being revealed to me. The sun beamed brightly through a small crack in the blinds, focusing directly on my face. It seemed inescapable; no matter how I tossed or turned it would follow. The sun, gently reminding me with its warm rays, that it was well beyond time to crawl from this bed. My sore and runny eyes slowly peeled apart to greet this midday sun; my mind racing to try to make sense of its surroundings. "How the hell did I get home," I thought to myself as I realized I was in my own bed. Glancing over, I noticed a small patch of blonde and brown hair buried within the fluffy white blankets. Tracing it backwards I quickly came to realize that it belonged to my girlfriend; she must have driven me home. As I laid there staring up at the sharp and pointy textured ceiling, flashbacks of the night before started to hit me. I was instantly overcome with a sense of panic that was quickly replaced with guilt and shame.

I spiraled, and I spiraled hard. My inauthenticity was catching up to me, and my lies were proving to have unintended consequences. I was learning the hard way; I would ultimately learn the hard and the long way. A life of constant covering and the inability to be one's self was resulting in a festering depression. A growing and nagging sadness that would not stop following me; an ailment that I had thus far crutched with alcohol and by turning a blind eye. An unrecognized shadow-creature that followed me everywhere that I would go; one that would continue to follow me for many years. I was living a life that grew less desirable to live with each passing day. At the time, none of this was visible. I approached any potential solutions for entirely the wrong reasons. I could not connect the dots that I was numbing because I was hiding away massive portions of who I was meant to be. I could not pinpoint that this nagging sadness came from years of self-suppression. I could not comprehend that partying was a distraction; a tool that I used to keep my mind at bay. By now, I had long given up on the idea of ever coming out. Honestly, it rarely even crossed my mind, it seemed like pure fantasy. I could not give up this life of pretend that I had spent so many years constructing; coming out and being myself wasn't an option that was on the table. I could not take the risk of being "othered," and I could not lose my friends and family. I thought that my only option was to continue this life of faux happiness by doubling-down on what I knew, fitting in and fitting in well. I would continue to float for some months to come, and I would face many more ups and downs during these months. I would find myself as the crying and depressed drunk, I would catch my mask slipping from time to time, and no matter how loudly every fiber of my being would scream, "just be yourself," I would push back against it that much harder.

Sometimes life just works out; opportunity meets fate and you get lucky. After floating and floating, I would eventually find opportunity within the profession of my late father. I would drop out of college and begin traveling; this was not a bad life for a young man. I would pick up where dad left off, working from power plant to power plant, and moving from state to state. This opportunity was great, but it extended well beyond monetary compensation and free sightseeing. This was a chance to run away, even if it was only for a few months at a time. This was an opportunity for change and was my chance at survival. My newfound career was the break that I so desperately needed, it would break the cycle, it would pull me from my state of limbo, and it would buy me a little more time. I packed up that old faded-black Ford F-150 one day, dad's old truck that had now become mine, and I was off. I traveled most of the east coast, going as far west as Vicksburg Mississippi. I'd spend all the spring and winter months chasing work, working outages in nuclear power plants. Power plants usually reserve major maintenance activities for non-peak times such as the spring and fall months. Winter and summer were strictly off-limits; the plants needed to remain operating to meet the demand created by those harsher months. As much as I thought that I had escaped, I had not. I had only bought my self some precious moments away; I had only found something else to momentarily distract myself.

Work had become my new party; it was my latest outlet. Only with work, no one would really complain when I poured myself into it for hours on end. All this over-achieving eventually led to some recognition and ended up with me starting a new career in industrial safety. This newly discovered profession would keep me running the roads for a bit longer as I gained experience and some education. But this added opportunity was just that much more of an excuse to attempt to kill myself with work; attempts that my employers quite appreciated. My near suicidal work ethic and sleep patterns did eventually payoff; life is funny in that way. I was working my fingers to the bone to forget who I was, not to become great at something. I was fortunate enough that it did both for me.

The cabin of the car erupted with a loud and resonate rumble as I drifted across the line and onto the apron of the road. The loose gravel and sand showered the undercarriage of my *Challenger*. "How do people drive on roads this damn straight," I thought to myself as I gently pulled my car back into alignment with the faded lane markings. The warm sun poured through my un-tinted glass of the windscreen and directly into my lap, warming my legs to the point of discomfort. I was stiff, I was tired, and I was done with driving. I had just spent the last two days on the road; stopping only long enough to sleep. I had spent the last 48 hours surviving on a mixture of stale trail mix, acetaminophen, near caustic gas station coffee, and *The Velvet Underground*. The drive had been amazing thus far and I had gotten to see so much of the country that I had long feared I would never see. Two days prior, I had embarked on this sacred journey. A journey that townie kids often daydream of while examining their bleak existences. This had been a daydream that I had dreamt on many occasions; one that I was now fortunate enough to turn to reality. I was lucky; life had finally dealt me a good hand. I was driving from coast to coast – well nearly. My final stop would be Arizona; a near-Martian land compared to the Virginia hills that I knew well. I would end my days of driving approximately 1,985 miles from where I had started this journey; 1,985 miles away from anything that I knew. I found myself undertaking this long mission in support of my newly discovered career path. I had shined bright as a young professional; I had continued to pour my heart and soul into my vocation. A full-time position awaited me in Phoenix, and I started in just a few days.

"Things have never been this bad; what the hell is wrong with this country?" he said. The words rolled from his lips unabridged, "it's not like the good ole' days anymore! Our country has fallen from grace with god!" he explained while addressing the small crowd. "These gays can just do whatever they please; the world is full of so much sin and they are the worst of it. That's the reason we're in such a mess!" he continued. "We're just supposed to accept all this sin and shut up? There is an active assault against us god-fearing good people these days." This Westboro Baptist style rant was not from an extremist preacher; it did not take place in a backwoods church house in some distant hollow. This was not the ramblings of some lunatic on a street corner with a bible and a megaphone; this was not a member of some fundamentalist group spewing hate at some rally. His words continued to bounce from the surrounding windows and walls with a slight echo, "We need to move back towards god and put these sinners in their place! That's the only way forward!" he finally concluded. "Alright, lets get down to the 3$^{rd}$ quarter reports," he said while thumbing through the stack of slides in front of him. Stunned, I melted into my chair and stared a hole through the adjacent egg-shell colored wall. "It's inescapable," I thought to myself; my mind was flooded with flashbacks to similar observations of such shallow mindedness. I was a couple of years into my new life; Arizona had been good to me so far. Life was getting better and I was discovering pieces of myself that I couldn't have found in Virginia. Though minute, I was making some progress towards finding out a little bit more about who I was.

Work was always the great unknown; now it was no longer that unknown. That which I had feared to be true, had now shown its ugly self quite clearly. During my earlier days as a grunt in this industry, I would hear a whisper of this or rumor of that. I would observe a random homophobic comment or slur from time to time; something muttered under someone's breath. Most, if not all, seemed to be quite random and kind of rare actually. It all seemed to matter much less than this; this was coming from a decision maker. These comments, these beliefs, were coming from a senior-level leader in one of the industry's largest companies. There it was again, that hot, prickly, cold, and sweaty feeling. With each step that I would take forward, it seemed that bigoted and backwards mindsets would quickly erase my progress. I would again let the mindsets of others have dominion over me; I had done this for years. I was not brave, and I was far from courageous. The need for self-preservation far outweighed the need for self-acceptance. The more time that I spent in my trade, the more that I would discover that these mindsets lingered at all levels of organizations. My fears, the ones that I thought I could outrun, had flooded back into my body. My most recent of observations reignited all the worries of my youth. They mixed and melded together with these new experiences to form some new grander version of self-rejection.

I was raised to firmly understand that different was bad; I was taught to abhor uniqueness. I carried these lessons with me, I carried them far from where they had originated. I discovered that there was no amount of distance that could simply erase them; they were scarred on to my mind. Worse yet, I had not only brought these with me, but I discovered that they had red-neck cousins in Arizona. Though they lived 1,985 miles away, these ideas were just as misguided and ignorant as the ones I had grown up with. When these two worlds finally collided, I was the one stuck in the middle. My Arizona honeymoon had come to an abrupt end. When east met west, and when work met personal, rather than leaning in, I ran towards the security of self-rejection. I willfully accepted that deeply visceral need of self-preservation; that primal desire for survival overtook my life. A new and old bitter concoction of misinformation, religious propaganda, and fear, all came together to ensure that I would not seek to embrace this uniqueness that I was gifted. I pushed it farther down, I swore-off my desires, and I drove my feelings in harder than ever before. I prayed to some silent and looming god to kill this part of me. This part of me, a part that I never had any say in, one that only brought me torment and a nagging ache. This god would not hear me, and I could not see beyond my need for survival. I was again stuck; I had simply picked up and moved my personal purgatory from Virginia to Arizona.

The dark and cold room began to glow with a pale yellowish light. The light shined from a distant table and up the wall; brightly illuminating the ceiling above. The warm glow was soon followed with a loud and panicked digital roar, a mixture of vibration and ringing. It was 4:30 AM and it was time to get up; it was time to go to work. I poured myself from the warm comfort of the bed and into the room's cool and crisp morning air. My body near immediately showing its disapproval; my skin responding with chill bumps. I rushed my way through my ritualistic morning routine, jumped into the nearest clean clothes I could find, and rushed out the door. The crisp and cold conditioned air of my house was quickly replaced with the warm and dry natural Arizona air. The dry warmth surrounded me as I made my way towards a large and shiny work truck in my driveway. Using the steering wheel, I pulled myself from the concrete driveway up, and into the cab. My day officially started, and I was on my way.

The once lunar-like landscaped now passed before me without thought as I navigated through the rush hour traffic. I had spent a couple of weeks in Virginia some months prior; I had been there for the holidays. As I stood there admiring the snow-covered hills and mountains that had surrounded my youth, their beauty struck me. I never realized how amazingly beautiful that small town was until I left. The shocking beauty of the southwest had now become my normal; Virginia was now the rarity. The experience was reversed, and the desert was now my home. I had been back attending the Christmas festivities, visiting family, and seeing my most recent of girlfriends. We had met a while back when I was first traveling around the country; we had been doing this for a while. We were locked in a dance of an on-again, off-again relationship that we had developed over a couple of years. During my visit, we were yet again on, spending some of the trip together. As much as I enjoyed my time in Virginia, it was good to be back home and on my own.

I continued my commute; embattled in a war against I-10 traffic. I eventually made it across town and to my office for the day, a dusty old jobsite trailer. I spent the first few minutes unpacking my backpack and trying to get the antique projector to function with my more modern laptop. I would be spending the entire day teaching classes to new employees; workers that the company had hired for an upcoming project. Soon the room was filled with rough and gruff construction workers, all that would rather be working than listening to my spiel on workplace health and safety. We pressed on and we managed to put a decent sized dent into the massive slide deck that we were required to complete. As we returned from a quick coffee break, I felt a slight "bzzzz," in my pocket. A quick glance at my phone revealed a text from my currently "on again" girlfriend. I pushed my phone back into my pocket without reading it and resumed teaching; time was of the essence. No one, including myself, had any intentions of staying late. As I continued from slide to slide, droning on and on about corporate bull shit, I could feel my phone continuing to vibrate. It's attempts to win my attention would not be successful, if I kept going at this rate we'd be done early. I continued to ignore its nagging "bzzz-

bzzz," as I pressed on through the bland presentation. Eventually we were done and due to our unwavering attention, we finished an hour early. An hour that I was ecstatic to reclaim, I was ready to call it a day. After breaking down and packing up, I could finally turn some attention to my phone. I had several missed calls and texts; opening her texts revealed her urgent pleas. She had repeatedly asked, "give me a call as soon as you can." I tossed my bag to the ground beside the door and took a seat. I gently eased down into a plastic folding chair, it creaked and groaned under my weight. I pulled myself up to the matching plastic foldup table and made the call. "Hey!" she answered energetically. "What's up?" she continued. "Not a lot, just wrapping up for the day. What's going on?" I replied inquisitively. "Are you sitting down?" she inquired. My stomach instantly dropped, and my mind ventured to the worst of places. "Oh no, who's dead?" I thought to myself. After a long and tense pause, a few short breaths that felt like a few years, she finally blurted it out: "I'm pregnant."

# Revelations

I stood there solemnly staring out into the dark blue oblivion. My feet were planted firmly in the mountains of sand beneath them. I could feel the sharp and rough edges rubbing between my toes; each almost microscopic grain of sand screaming at me to run. The cool winds blowing in from the Pacific pushed firmly against me, telling me to go. My stomach was in knots, pleading with me to change my mind with each of its roaring growls. Even the seagulls with their caws and squawks, seemed to be telling me to turn back now and disappear into the San Diego streets. But it was all for nothing; I had come too far to turn back. This was what was supposed to come next; it was the only solution. I had long ago accepted my fate and I was now preparing to meet it. I knew what I had to do; it was almost over. Like ripping off a band aid, I just needed to get it over with quickly. And just like that, it happened: "I do." The preacher swiftly and with a smile shouted, "I now pronounce you husband and wife." Tears poured from me; this was a rare moment in which I cried uncontrollably. At the time, I chocked it up to joy or happiness. Crying is simply what one does during moments like this, during moments of extreme joy or overwhelming sadness. It is a normal human response to cry at events such as weddings and funerals. Looking back, I was sobbing because I knew deep down that this was the latter.

Things had gotten serious since the big news; life had taken on a completely new meaning. I was a young man who, in a short amount of time, would be a young father. That is not something that most would take lightly. I had grown up with amazing and positive male influence in my life; I had a father who embodied all that which is positive in that distinction. The importance of being a great father was apparent to me; I knew its weight long before I'd officially have the title. This was not like other events in my life; I could not just pretend that it was not happening. I could not just push my head into the sand to avoid it. In a truly short matter of time, I would be a dad. I was ecstatic to get to be a father; I had wanted kids for as long as I could remember. This was a gift, and I was happy to receive it. Upon discovering the news, I was overwhelmed with joy and happiness. I could not wait to meet this little thing; something that was made of me. My own flesh and blood manifesting before my own eyes; something made of my own image. Being a dad is something that I had long dreamed of, a dream that I would now get to witness come true.

In addition to the responsibilities of my upcoming fatherhood, I felt as if I needed to "do the right thing." I had to perform some valiant and chivalrous act of yesteryear; I had to marry the person that now carried my child. In attempts to live up to some mixture of small-town morals and religious doctrine, I married her that day. Please do not take this the wrong way or misconstrue my words; I put a lot in to being married. I honestly tried as hard as I could to make it work. Look, I am not going to make a bunch of bull shit excuses here. I should have never gotten married in the first place; in retrospect this is obvious. I was an ass hole who misled myself into believing that this was for the best. Worse yet, I misled a decent and good person into loving me. All the stupid things that we do as humans are obvious with the gifts of hindsight and known outcome. Unfortunately, our stupidity is usually not revealed to us until well after the fact. I had rushed into a shotgun wedding foolhardily trying to live up to some stupid code of chivalry. In doing so, I had become just another closeted gay man that was stuck in a straight marriage. But I had chosen this path, and I was trying to walk it to the best of my ability. This wasn't just some fake image anymore; I wasn't just pretending. I was married to a woman and had a child on the way. I wanted to be straight; I tried to be straight. I hoped each day that I would wake up a changed man. As if one morning my eyes would spring open to greet the day and I would suddenly realize that I had lost any appetite for men; that I now found them absolutely repulsive. I no longer just wanted to pretend to be someone else, I wanted to change. I was so worn down and tired of living that fake life, a totally hopeless life now that I was stuck with my ill-advised marriage, that I would beg any god that I thought might listen. I wanted to be straight, I wanted to be a good husband, and most of all, I wanted to be a great dad. I mistakenly assumed that these three were one and the same; that I could not be great at one without the others. I convinced myself that each of these categories were interlocked and dependent upon one another. If I were not straight, my marriage would not work. If my marriage did not work, how could I be a great dad? I was living the image that I was told I was supposed to live, some beautiful straight portrait of normal. A picture that someone else had designed for my life long ago, a husband, a wife, a baby, a dog, and a house. I lived that life the best that I could, for as long as I could. Despite all my efforts, nothing really changed. Who I was never actually went away, and my prayers were never answered. As time would pass, I would drift farther into my own mind, examining the things that could have been. My thoughts would run wild and I would often drift into visions of another life, looking down from some god-like perch upon an existence that could have been. I was observing some other dimension in which everything was different; a world in which I was out and in a relationship with some imaginary man. It was the same but different. The perfect picture in my head did not match the one that I had. Husband, husband, baby, dog, and house would often float across my thoughts. I was peering down upon a life in which I was happy.

I would imagine the mundane; these small little tidbits of the day that most take for granted. I would daydream about things as boring as grocery shopping with him. I would slip off to some parallel universe where I would be doing laundry and folding his boxers. I would vividly fantasize about his arms wrapping around me, his smell, and the feeling of his skin against mine as we would lay in bed drifting to sleep. I would imagine my head buried in his chest with my legs wrapped around him, laying on the couch watching some dumb movie. It was in these momentary glimpses of the life that I so desired, that I finally realized an earth-shattering truth. I had a monumental moment of clarity; I was blessed with a realization that I had long needed. I could never genuinely love a woman. I had tried and tried, to no avail. Year over year, I was hoping to "fix" myself; doing my best to cover the things that I thought were wrong with me. Giving it my all to prevent the intrusion of onlookers, keeping their curious eyes and questions away from my true self. I must have thought that if I could only pretend long enough then it would finally take; that I could "fake it until I could make it." If I could only pretend to be straight long enough, I would wake up straight one day. With each passing year and each new layer of cover, the exact opposite was true. My soul was on fire; every fiber of my being was screaming out at me in agony. With each escalating step, steps that had now landed me wedlocked, the need to be true to myself was magnified. During these miniscule moments of imagination, something finally clicked into place. Some primordial piece of my brain finally awakened, revealing to me the truth. No matter how hard I tried, it was impossible for me to romantically love a woman. I was wired differently; I finally accepted that.

Is it nature? Is it nurture? Is it both? Sure. The way that I ended up becoming my unique self didn't really matter all that much now. I had finally started to understand that this was me; this was never changing. This was an unwavering part of myself that had been with me since forever. I was awakening to the truth of the situation, that I was born and destined to be exactly this. Through this great revelation, I could begin the long and tedious journey of reconciling who I was, with who I needed to be. I could begin the process of prying into the catacombs of my mind and peeling apart the layers of my existence. I could now begin to deconstruct the mistruths that had been taught to me, I could work past my own flawed assumptions, and I could come to terms with a path forward for my life. I now started to see clearly; a veil had been lifted from my eyes. I could see now that being a great dad had nothing to do with being married; it had nothing to do with being straight or gay. I was awakened to the fact that the only way that I could ever be a great husband, was with a husband of my own. The elements contained within this grand portrait of life were not as interconnected as they appeared, at least not in the ways that I had originally imagined. With this acknowledgement, the pressure would now begin to mount. I had lit a fuse, I had started a timer, and it was just a matter of time. I could not hold onto this secret for much longer; there was a burning in my heart to scream the truth from roof top to roof top. There was now a yearning in my soul to share the real me with the world. But I couldn't come out to the world, at least not just yet. First, I had to tell my wife. I had to finally confess to her the truth; something that she had deserved since the first day that we met. Something that we both had deserved for a very long time.

A knot in my stomach that will not go away, a hole in my heart that I can't seem to mend, an endless sense of despair or dread, a feeling that I just couldn't seem to put my finger on. Depression is surprisingly hard to describe; it comes in many shapes and forms and these generic terms just never seem to do it justice. Some days I just couldn't get out of bed. Every now and then, I would break down for no apparent reason at all. Other times I would be smiling and laughing like everything was fine; you'd never know that I felt like my heart was being clawed out of my chest. I knew these feelings well, I had known them for many years, but I was never quite aware of what they were until more recently. Depression had first introduced itself to me when I was a much younger man. But mental health, much like sexuality, was not something that was on the table for discussion during my childhood. Are you sad? That's an easy fix, we'll pray those depression demons right out of you. You think you are gay? That's an easy fix, we'll pray those gay demons right out of you, and you'll be good as new! As much as I would like to say I'm joking, I'm not totally. I vividly recall a memory of a church sermon in which depression was attributed to some form of demonic possession. In the very same sermon, this backwoods preaching went as far as blaming the individual for "letting worldly things corrupt them," leading to their depression. Who the hell is going to raise their hand and say, "I think I'm sad and I might need help," if there's a very real chance that you will be blamed and publicly exercised for doing so? Silence was a good rule to live by when growing up around religious extremism; it is the real golden rule of Christianity. I was taught that silence was a virtue, and I continued to carry this virtue with me. But silence sucks when you're in the real world. I now know what that knot in my stomach was; back then it was just another flaw to add to my long list of things that ailed me. Even though I was much more aware during this more recent bout with this "demon," I completely lacked the knowledge of how to deal with it. Awe shucks backwoods views on mental health and depression, thanks for not teaching me anything! I did know one thing that I needed to do; something that would ease my burden. I needed to start the process of truth telling. I needed to come out. I was stuck, knowing what I needed to do without taking any action to do it. I was scared and I was trying to build up the courage to face this fear. The longer I waited the worse that it would get. Lies do not age well, they only fester and become more repulsive over time. I couldn't keep up the lie any longer; it was time to finally get honest.

"I think he is kind of cute," I casually mentioned to her; adding my two cents to a discussion about an actor in a film that we were watching. We were in the bedroom of our recently purchased home; tucked behind a white picket fence in a quaint suburban neighborhood. We were watching some dumb romantic comedy and folding clothes as we set on the end of the bed. This is probably not something most men say to their wives, you are probably thinking at this point. You see, I was breaking the ice. I was testing the waters to see if they were safe to enter. I was trying to ease into a hard conversation about the truth. How do you come out to someone that you're married to? How do you tell someone that you are supposed to love, that you cannot love them in the way that they need? How do you tell your spouse the news that will bring your union to its conclusion? There are no simple answers to those questions, as I would soon discover. "You think he's cute, huh?" she said; responding to my seemingly playful banter. "He's pretty hot actually," I said with a slight chuckle. "Shut up!' she responded with a laugh. "No really, I think he's super attractive," I said in a more pointed tone. She looked at me puzzled; peering deeper to see if I was joking. "Like you think he's sexy in…. what kind of way?" she said. "Are you just acknowledging his level of attractiveness, or are you actually attracted to him?" she continued. After pausing momentarily, I said, "I am totally attracted to him; I am kind of attracted to men." I witnessed the confusion on her face grow; quickly turning from playful to bewildered. The dialogue continued back and forth, only confirming the truth that I had already revealed. I shared with her some of my secrets, telling of certain encounters that I had experienced throughout my life. I was skirting around the "G" word; I was just avoiding it out of fear. Even so, I was slowly coming clean, and it felt fucking amazing! Our conversation suddenly stopped; people tend to grow quiet when they do not know what to say next. A deafening silence overtook the room, "Ok, I get it that you are attracted to men. But what exactly does that mean?" My heart raced, it was beating so fast and hard that you could almost visibly see it through my shirt. "Fuck, this is it," I thought to myself. I was finally going to do it; I was just a few words away from the freedom of unabridged truth. I gazed down upon my bare feet against the dark hardwood floor; trying to formulate the best possible response that I could. I was tugging at my fingers and became lost deep in thought; "I'm... um... I," I barely managed to squeeze out before abruptly cutting myself off. "What the hell do I say? I am about to break her heart," I thought while trying to find the perfect words. "I – I – I... I'm, I'm, I'm... Bi." I finally pushed out. I was instantly overcome with shame; I had again lied. I had yet again covered who I really was, only to a lesser degree. "What the fuck is wrong with me," I whispered to myself. I could see her panic and confusion quickly fade; like she had dodged the bullet of having a gay husband. I guess that was sort of the point, but in my panicked attempt to deaden the blow, I had only delayed the inevitable. In my efforts to go easy, I had only made things much worse in the long run.

"Where do I go from here?" I thought to myself as I stared up at the slightly off-white ceiling of our bedroom. It was nearing noon on a Saturday; a beautiful Phoenician day awaited me outside. The sunny and warm day just outside of my windows, was a day of which I wanted no part in. I rolled myself tighter in the thick down comforter as I continued to stare up at the ceiling deep in thought. I could hear the muffled sounds of yardwork taking place through the neighborhood; the sporadic buzzing of mowers and trimmers all screaming at me for remaining in bed. The busy world outside could wait; I had no place in that world. In the months following my artificial coming out, this had become a normal occurrence. I would work as much as I possibly could; clocking as many hours as my employer would allow. After work, I would run home, change clothes, and would disappear to the gym for another several hours. Upon finally returning home for the night, I would pour myself back into the soft cool bed where I had started my day. On the weekends, I would try my best to work. Though, that was usually not an option. So, I would spend as much of those days as I could wrapped up in bed. Rolled up tightly in that cool down comforter with only my head emerging; this would either become my cocoon or my coffin.

My depression had now become crippling; I was nearing the point of becoming non-functional. The minute slivers of any remaining hope had departed from my body many months prior. Melancholy and hopeless is a dreadful place to reside; each moment lived in this horrible state pushes one nearer to the brink of nothingness. This mixture of sadness and despair can push a person to unthinkable notions. It was from this desolate abyss that I concluded that I had only two choices before me. I could no longer continue to navigate this balance beam between two lives; tiptoeing across a wall that separated who I was, and who I was supposed to be. I could no longer split the difference between the life I had and the life I needed. I had only two choices; there was now an obvious fork in my path. I could either live or die. I could live the life I was born to live or bring the one I had to its obvious and needed conclusion. I finally found the end of the maze; I had finally pushed myself to the point of extreme clarity. I had reduced this grand and complex situation to its two simplest choices: life or death. I had a frightening amount of calmness with this proposition; either selection would bring me peace. For as long as I could remember, being at peace had been the only true goal.

This was the first time that my mind had wandered into these deep and dark waters; it would not be the last. As I spent some time contemplating my choices, the true weight of those selections came crashing down upon me. A choice between life and death, is no real choice at all. The life that I needed was waiting for me, all I had to do was act. My long-held fantasy did not have to remain in my head as a daydream; my actions could change my life for the better. For all of the things that pushed me into this hole, I had just as many reasons to claw my way out of it. I was a father; the thought of leaving my daughter stopped me dead in my tracks. I was fortunate to have a large family and amazing friends. My heap of positives greatly outweighed my pile of pain; I had much to live for. I was lucky enough to awaken to this fact before it was too late. It's quite easy to investigate the world of a deeply depressed and hopeless person and think, "Why don't they just do something different?" Hell, it's easy for me to look back on my own life and say the same, but it's never quite as easy as it seems. The pain and despair festers and grows like a cancer on your soul; pain only leading to more pain. A self-perpetuating sadness that only multiplies and worsens until something finally snaps within you! I was lucky to say the least; many are not here to share this story. I had now made my choice and I was ready to take action. As horrible and fucked up as it sounds, my brush with self-destruction granted me clarity that I had never before experienced. I now knew what I wanted; I wanted to live. I did not want to live some bull shit excuse of a life, I did not want to lead the life that I was told I was supposed to lead, I wanted to live the life I was born to live. In some last-ditch effort, my brain had simplified the complex situation that I had lived with for so long. My mind had given me two simple, yet extreme choices. My life had devolved to a choice between life and death, and I had finally made the choice to live. I had made the choice to emerge from this cocoon, rather than choosing it to be my coffin.

After a couple years of marriage and months of numbing depression, I finally confessed the full truth to my then wife. It went about as well as you can imagine; I never assumed that it would be easy. When a straight woman suddenly realizes that she has married a gay man, its chocked full of tears and heartbreak. It is a process of many ups and downs, to say the least. As painful and hard as it was to finally reveal the full truth to her, it instantaneously lifted a weight from my shoulders. In the long run, it would lift a burden from her as well. She gained a deeper understanding of the issues our relationship faced; our ailments were incurable because we were incompatible. You sometimes do not realize the burden that you are carrying until its gone; now feeling the lightness in your step and recognizing regained speed that you had lost long ago. Describing the abatement of depression, is nearly as hard has describing its symptoms. I felt like a new person; I felt as if I had started the process of healing. I came to grander realizations about myself and my life. I now understood that to be the amazing father that I so desired to be, that I had to be me. To be a great dad, I had to first accept myself and get better. I could clearly see the path forward for my life; a path to happiness I had not yet known. These great revelations, and many more, were only revealed to me upon the lifting of this weight. It was like the sun had finally fought its way through the clouds; its warm rays shining down upon me. I felt like I had a crushing weight removed from my chest and could finally breathe. When I smiled, it was because I meant it. Hope had returned to my life; flooding and filling the void that despair had left. It was like I had lived my life in shackles, and they had finally been removed. It was like I had been born again.

# Born Again

Coming out just sort of happens. There does not seem to be some magical and perfect sequence of actions; must-do's that domino one after another leading to some logical conclusion. It all just seems to happen when it's supposed to happen. The whole process feels chaotic, messy, and somewhat random. I would love to be able to give some grand advice on this subject, but there are no clear-cut answers. Your truth is yours and yours alone; its your choice as to when and if you would like to share that truth. It is your right to choose who you would like to share your truth with, and when you would like to share it. I waited until I was in my mid-twenties, married with a child, and mortgage in hand, before I finally spilled my guts. I wish that I could give you an all-inclusive guide to coming out; something that would take away all your anxiety and fears. I wish that I had all the answers for allies on how to support those that you love; how to help your family and friends with this process and how to support them in speaking their own truth. Sadly, I do not possess these answers; I've grown to believe over the years that no one does. So, this is not a guide on escaping the closet or some bull shit, "10 steps to acceptance" book. This is not "25 proven and easy ways to love your gay son!" or anything even remotely close. Life is entirely too nuanced for me to give broad and sweeping advice on such an important and delicate subject. I am not some gay shaman; I am not your queer guru. I am not the person that should be giving coming out advice, so I won't. I am also not going to soapbox or make demands on how to best support your LGBTQ+ friends and family members. But I will leave you with one small piece of advice; a thread that I hope to weave throughout this book: Treat people how you would like to be treated. I will also share with you some of my stories and how I dealt with the process. From these stories, I hope that you can distill down your own lessons and takeaways. I hope that I can shine a spotlight on the issues that many of us face; challenging perceptions around coming out and bringing much needed visibility to the topic. I hope that my stories and thoughts can help friends and family members fill the gaps in support that commonly exist; that they might bring you support if you are venturing down the path of coming out or know someone that is.

In my case, it took me around 25 years to come completely "out." I came out to a person here and a person there, swearing them to secrecy or death. When I finally decided to give my truth to the world, it came with a mixed bag of reactions. Coming out came with blowback. I cannot tell you that coming out will be easy, and I will be the last one to try to push you to do it before you're ready. Examining my own life makes me realize that I came out when it was finally safe for me to do so; it happened when it was supposed to. If I would have busted

down the door of my childhood home and loudly and

proudly screamed, "Hey y'all! I'm gay!" I would have swiftly been kicked right back out of that door I had just marched through. I would have been homeless for simply admitting who I really was. I can say with reasonable certainty that I would have been exiled to the streets, or I would have been sent off to one of those creepy Christian fundamentalist gay conversion camps. So yeah, it was not safe for me to come out. I had to choose between shutting up or being homeless. I was forced to pick from being "straight," or having some deeply closeted pastor electrocute my testicles in a shed in the woods somewhere. There is not much choice in situations like that. I was not ready to speak my truth, so I kept it hidden. The environment in which I found myself was not conducive to truth telling; honesty was not possible. So, I chose to be dishonest and I sought self-preservation over self-expression. The world that I was raised in did not allow for any truth other than gods truth. Looking back, I probably made the right choice at the time. I must tell you, that is not an easy thing to say. I'll also admit that I took covering much too far, obviously. This mixture of backwoods biblical philosophy, small-town shallow mindedness, and my own fears and blind spots, always made coming out appear to be pure fantasy. Living a life true to myself never seemed to be possible until now. I finally found myself ready, willing, and in the right environment to remove my worn and ragged mask. I was ready to drop my cover and live the life I was meant to live.

My stomach was on fire; every anxious and nervous feeling that I had ever experienced seemed magnified ten-fold. I was barely clinging to consciousness as I pecked away at the chipped and cracked screen of my phone. I was chasing the right words, though they seemed just out of my grasp. My heart was pounding like a drum, my respirations rhythmically following suit. I dug my toes into the soles of my shoes in some odd attempt to keep from falling off the earth. I felt as if I could be thrown from my earthly home and flung into the heavens at any moment; a quick flick of gods hand knocking me into the cold blackness. "This is supposed to be the easy one," I thought to myself as I continued to stare at my empty message. I was searching for the words to tell my youngest sister that I had spent a lifetime hiding from her who I really was. We were always close; being so alike made us that much closer. I had made up my mind in the weeks leading up to this nausea inducing coming out party, that she would be the first in my family to know. I had longed for years to tell her; I needed her help for what was to come next. My eyes were glazed over, my mind in deep contemplation. I set there in the early morning darkness of my car continuing to search for the right words. The stillness of daybreak was only interrupted by the light chirping of birds and the occasional passing car. My time was not limitless as I had to depart for work, or risk being late. The pressure was beginning to mount; I had to do this now. I couldn't keep it in any longer. I would not allow myself to put this off yet again.

As the pressure continued to build, I rapidly fired off a message, a warning shot: "I have something big to tell you," I typed and instantly sent. I waited there in the dead silence of my car for what felt like hours, receiving her response near moments after my originating message. "Ok, what's going on?" she replied. "I really need to tell you something," I wrote. "Tell me?" she quickly typed back. "I'm trying... I just can't get it out..." I responded. We went back and forth for several rounds: her asking and me not telling. Eventually I caved; I couldn't hold back that burning truth one moment longer. What had been so complicated and miserable was now reduced to one simple and clean statement of fact: "I'm gay." I typed those words and sent them as fast as my fingers would allow. Near instantly the light of my phone again illuminated the morning darkness. It was her response; her name brightly lit across my phone. I nervously gazed at the screen, fearful to open the message and view her reaction. My curiosity finally got the better of me. With a quick swipe and a short passcode, I could see her response: "Fuck you!" she had replied. My heart sank and melted into the floorboard of my car. Her response

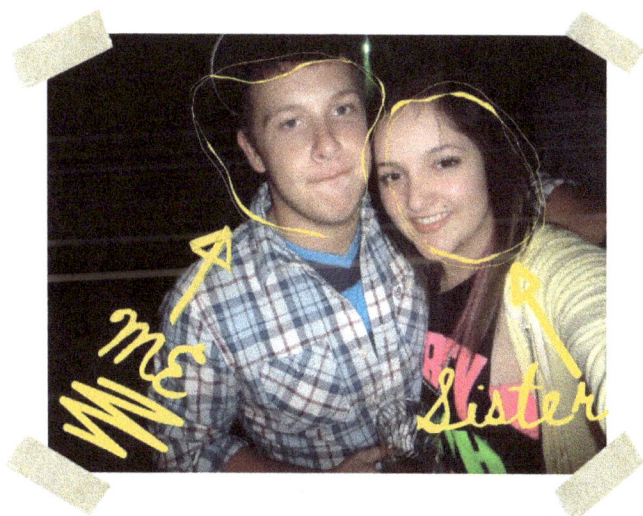

was not nearly as bad as it sounds. I knew this "fuck you;" she thought that I was joking. She believed that this had all been some elaborate prank that I had played on her. "No really, I'm not joking. I am gay…" I replied. The tone of our conversation shifted, moving from frustration to curiosity and onto concern. It then evolved into love and support upon the realization of the magnitude of what I was confessing to her. I can't quite recall how she exactly responded to my big news after the understanding that it was not a prank. Much of this interaction became a blur, an obscured image in my head with brief moments of sharp and extreme clarity. But I do know the tone of our conversation; she was loving and supportive. She was exactly what I needed her to be in that moment, in my moment of extreme vulnerability.

There always seems to be some sense of betrayal; people that you come out to always feel misled. Even with the most supportive of allies, there always appears to be some tinge of the feelings of disloyalty. With more supportive folks, it probably comes from the fact that they feel like you should have told them. They knew their level of support for you; they assumed that you knew their level of support. The opposite group of people, those that are a little less onboard with who you are, take your personal truth as almost a personal slight. These people are probably a significant portion of the reason why many of us remain in the closet for so long.

These non-supportive acquaintances are the misguided, the bigoted, the homophobic, the religious zealots, and the like. They view us as a contradiction to their world views, an abomination against some magic book, or an insult to their own belief system. You will find that everyone you tell will feel some sense of betrayal in the process. After the realization that I was dead serious, my sister fully supported me. But I could feel that she was confused as to why I never told her; she felt that I should have said something sooner. I think most can appreciate that response and can fully respect those feelings when they are had for the right reasons. The problem lies with one simple fact: you never know how people really feel. You will never know how they will react, until they react. Those that have never held the fear of being something other than what is expected of them seem to struggle with that notion. People will surprise you. You will come across homophobes hiding in plain sight; people that you would assume to be supportive quickly prove themselves to be the opposite. You will receive support and love in places that you would least expect it; extremely religious people that will love and accept you with open arms. Coming out acts as a magnifying glass upon the belief systems of those that you confide in; you will find some jaw-dropping contradictions. You never really know how people feel until you muster up the courage to say those simple little words: "I am gay." When it was all said and done, and after multiple heart to hearts, I was officially out to the first member of my family. I was out to her and coming out went surprisingly well, well enough to energize me for the next several bouts with this repetitious and grueling process. I was energized and now had a much-needed ally on my side.

"But you are not like the girl, right?" she responded after I had just spent the last 30-minutes of my existence pouring out my heart and soul to her. This was the second official family member on my list; I had just come out to an aunt that I was very close to. I want to press pause right here for just a moment. Look, I know I said that I wasn't going to give any advice; I even kind of made a big deal about that at the beginning of this chapter. But let me say this, that is never an appropriate question to ask a queer person. Everyone say it with me: "I will never ask a gay man, or any member of the LGBTQ+ community for that matter, if they are the man or the woman in the relationship." You can claim ignorance once; I'll personally give you one pass. But if you continue to ask that question, you my friend are an asshole. She did not mean anything by it; this response just sort of came out. To her, and to a lot of people, it seems like the logical next question. I wasn't offended or hurt by the comment, it just threw me for a loop. It knocked me off my game; it killed my momentum. What the hell do you even say to that? At this point I had barely expressed that I was gay, I had just revealed a secret that I had carried for 25 years, and now I was going to have to explain my sexual position to a close family member? After a few moments spent in apparent disbelief, I responded with the first thing that came to my mind. "I'm a gay man...I like men... there is not a woman in that equation. It is just two men, that's the entire point." Her comment was not meant to be hurtful; it wasn't hurtful to me if I'm being completely transparent. My response to her question seemed to flip a switch and bring about some level of understanding. Even without ill-intent, it shines a bright light on a big problem; it exposes a bias that many of us hold. It demonstrates a complete and utter lack of understanding, and common misguided beliefs around human sexuality.

Allow me to translate, "But you are not like the girl, right?" into an easier to understand question. This loosely translates to: "You are entirely too masculine to be a bottom. Because you are masculine that means you must be the pitcher rather than the catcher, right?" Its connotation goes even farther to say, "I know you are gay, but at least you're not on the receiving end of things, because that would be really gay." Like this was some positive thing; I was gay but at least I wasn't that gay. Because of my masculinity, their bias had labeled me as "the man" in my future relations. Due to this, I was not shedding and destroying some bull shit level of manliness they had observed me having prior to coming out. This stereotype can go both ways and has been around since the dawn of time. Masculine men are men; feminine men are women! No matter how you slice this assumptive stereotype, its bull shit! I know that I have gone on a mini rant here, but it's an important one. So, please just bear with me and give me a moment. Stop labeling people based on their appearances, off their femininity or masculinity, and stop drawing broad assumptions about people in general. It is depressing, I couldn't tell you how many times I received this or some similar response: "You can't be gay… you're like a normal dude. You don't act all girly?" these are their words, not mine. You could write an entire book on this subject alone; I'm not going to write that book here. But just remember one of my first points; treat people how you would like to be treated. It is about time that we made the golden rule cool again! Do not form misguided assumptions about people and put them in the position of being hurt by your foolish assumptions. Allow people to tell you what they want to tell you and hold back what they choose to hold back. Maybe the rest of it, the other parts of their lives they withhold from you, are none of your business to begin with? Maybe I don't want to have to explain to my aunt what a bottom is? Maybe I shouldn't have to explain that there is not a woman in a relationship between two gay men? Maybe we should let people share what they want to share, and let them share it when they want to share it? Maybe we should be a little empathetic; treating people how we would want to be treated.

I need to come full circle here; this interaction was not negative at all. I use it as an example to draw attention to a problem, but overall, it was a good experience. I do not want to come across as offended, because I was not. Ignorance lacks intent; there was no blade in the comments that were made. There was no desire to inflict harm upon me or hurt me in anyway. Intent does matter and curiosity is not a bad thing.

Though, the questions asked can be a little archaic, at least they are being asked. This curiosity and questioning, even if a little clunky, leads to learning and a better understanding of the queer community. We need to talk more and be offended less; all of us can heed that advice. Through conversations we can make the world a better place for everyone. We can teach and expand minds, even if it's just in our circles of family and friends. After a few brief moments of disbelief, my aunt instantly accepted me. She welcomed me and my truth with open arms. I could not ask for more; she met my confession with love. She met my truth with understanding, with compassion, and with acceptance. Was she shocked by my abrupt disclosure? Most certainly. She, as so many others, had only ever known me as a straight man. I did everything to show her that I was the straightest person that she could possibly know. To her, and seemingly out of the blue, everything had suddenly changed. She had every right to be a little shocked by my admission. Coming out isn't just about expecting others to be understanding and accepting towards the person that is coming out. There must be understanding, acceptance, empathy, and love, flowing in both directions.

There was a common thread to the conversations that surrounded my adventures in truth telling. One reoccurring comment; a sharp question: "Have you told mom?" This question came up repeatedly. Some did not mince words, sharing a dire warning: "Do not tell mom." I remember these conversations vividly; these are those moments that become etched upon your brain. "You haven't told mom, yet have you?" I recall from one of these conversations. I had just come out to another family member, I had sobbingly poured out my heart and had shared my secret, and this was their most pressing concern. Upon revealing that I had not, I was met with a pointed comment on the topic, "Well don't, she's old and she just will not understand. This might kill her if you tell her the truth." I remember being flooded with anger; the notion of hiding who I was from anyone now pissed me off. Especially hiding from someone that I loved so dearly; it enraged me. I never had the opportunity to tell my father. I was not going to live with the same regret from not telling my mother. The conversation continued as I remained silent, stewing in my anger. "We'll just tell her that your marriage didn't work out. We can keep things under wraps, and she'll never know. Just don't get loose on social media with it and everything will be fine." I could not believe what I was hearing; I was being covered up. I could make out the words, but they did not make sense to me. I was being forcefully closeted; I was being hidden from my mom. I didn't have to worry about hiding any longer, they were going to do it for me. They were basically sentencing me to a continued life of concealment; never being able to say who I truly was. I would not be able to post a picture with a boyfriend on social media, I would not be able to admit going to a gay bar, or be able to wear a pride t-shirt, and for the remainder of my mother's natural life I would need to pretend to be straight. To me, that did not sound like a life worth living. I would rather be dead than live another day like that. That life was in stark contradiction to the choice that I had made to live! "Enough!" I shouted loudly. "It's not your choice, it's not your decision to make," I continued to say. "I'm telling her and that's final." There was some back and forth, but I quashed any ideas of hiding.

Some people will try to hijack your truth, they will attempt to commandeer your coming out, and they will demand authority over the process. I'm not talking about people offering some friendly advice; I am talking about those that attempt to pirate your truth. I had a handful of close family members and friends seek dominion over my truth telling. In my case, many tried to sway me from coming out to my mom. Others begged me to shut up, claiming that my sexuality would damage my reputation, send me to hell, or would destroy my future. Some of these people went as far as outing me to others; taking it upon themselves to share what was mine. I can't say this enough, this truth is yours alone. You will have hijackers; you must stop them dead in their tracks where you can. Do not allow others to dictate to you when you will come out, or who you will come out to. You will have those people, those that believe they know what is best, test your resolve. They will make demands and they will make a grab for control; only you have true control over what is happening. They can only gain dominance if you allow them. Do not give in and surrender something so precious. My anger saved me; years of pent up and suppressed rage protected me from these pirates. I would have none of it; the time for this bull shit was long gone. I lost some friends in the process, and some family members moved into the estranged category. Some retaliated by outing me early, and others just blocked me on social media. All of which was perfectly fine; I refused to allow them to take this from me. I refused to bend and break myself to fit into their mold. I refused to meet their demands. I no longer would allow anyone this type of control over me; I was determined to share my unredacted truth. My truth came before their perceived consequence.

There is not a right or wrong way to come out to someone. I came out to my sister through a text message, I came out to an aunt in person, I came out to a slew of others over the phone, and to some on *Facetime*. The right way, like the right timing, seems to reveal itself. I found myself facing the unique challenge of living 1,900 miles away from most of my friends and family. I was forced to get a little creative; those close to me were actually pretty far away. I just followed an unbalanced mixture of my gut and heart, making sure that they heard the truth from me first. For my mom, I wrote her a letter. It was fitting; she would often write us letters. Notes expressing her love towards us, or writings meant to guide us on a particular subject. Her beautiful cursive script filling a ruled piece of notebook paper; leaving us with tidbits of her wisdom. I set down one day, and I typed her a letter. I was at work and was in the midst of the daily afternoon lull. I was fortunate enough to have a small office; within it were two large windows directly behind my dated L-shaped desk. My office felt like a small, dark, chilly, and safe cave. The buildings more important inhabitants controlled its climate, its temperature was always set to a frosty "cold." I kept the fluorescent lights above me off most of the time; the windows were my primary light source. The suns warm rays cut through the cold air and wrapped around my back and shoulders; I set there for hours typing and editing this confession to perfection. I had no struggle finding the right words to say; the truth flowed from deep within me. I poured everything that I had into those pieces of paper, running on for 6 or so pages. When I started this project of coming out to my mother, I had envisioned mailing her this note. I wanted the process to be somewhat formal; I felt that an email would be too casual. Plus, I needed time to formulate and construct the best message that I could. So, a conversation was completely out of the question. I thought that a letter could be the best of both worlds; giving me time to gain clarity and meeting my needs of formality. But as my coming out compounded, there was chatter and talk about my revelation. I needed to get to her before someone else did; I needed to beat the gossip machine. I copied and pasted my work into an email. I set there staring at it blankly for some time; time seemed to slow as I evaluated what would come next. I rotated side to side in the squeaky old office chair that had been my home for the last several hours. I chewed on the end of an ink pen, rubbing my eyes with my free hand. All of my nervous "ticks" were manifesting all at once. I do not remember being anxious or actually feeling nervous for that matter. I remember feeling numb; I felt void of all emotions. This numbing was in preparation for what was to come; a response unlike any other I had received. Things were about to change; things would never be the same.

Distance can complicate things, but it can also shield from trauma. I honestly can't imagine how this entire process would have gone if I were local. I felt pretty fortunate during most of the process to live on the opposite side of the country. One extreme downside to coming out at a distance, is the waiting. It's absolutely miserable; a nerve-racking span of time that seems endless. Long nail-biting moments of extreme tension and worry; I would wish this disquieting time upon no person. I was waiting, the dim glow of my computer screen keeping me company in my lowly lit office. I stared at the lower-right corner of the screen, waiting for a chime and notification that she had responded. But nothing, and the minutes quickly turned to hours without a response. My nerves were shot, I was on edge, and the tension continued to mount, as I remained locked in my trance of watching and waiting. I waited and waited before it finally hit me: "She'll never see it!" I thought to myself. I quickly realized that she was likely to not check her email for days. "Fuck!" I said with frustration under my breath. I frantically started searching under the books and papers on my desk; I was looking for my phone. I must have knocked nearly everything to the floor during my hunt. Pens, pictures, papers, and books all fell to the floor as my search progressed. "My backpack!" I thought out loud. I had not taken my phone from my bag; up to this point my mind had been occupied with work and this gut-wrenching task. I ripped open my backpack with a quick tug on the zipper. There it was, I found my phone! I grabbed it and gave it a slight tap to bring it to life; nothing yet. She had most certainly not discovered my note.

I fumbled with the phone; my hands were shaking now with nervous woe. I managed to find her name and I pressed it. The phone came alive and the line started to trill; I was once again waiting on edge. Nothing, she did not answer. I quickly swiped back to the phones main screen and navigated my way to my messages. I scrolled and scrolled until I once again found her; I opened our conversation and started to type yet again. "Hey…" I typed and sent. I then followed up immediately with, "I sent you an email… please go take a look at it as soon as you can… please?!?" Coming out, especially at a distance, is long and nerve-racking blocks of silence with brief moments of sheer-panic sprinkled in. "Bzzz Bzzz," my phone emitted as it vibrated against the desk. "Ok, I'll go check it now" she had replied. Again, I was waiting. I felt more on edge during this 15 to 20-minute wait, than I ever had before. I felt like I was awaiting my execution; a crippling sense of dread overcame me.

My arms were crossed and resting on my desk; I was seated with my head buried in my crossed arms. A part of me wanted to lay down and die; I did not want to face what was coming. I wanted to crawl under my desk and disappear. I wanted to flee; to get in my car and drive until I ran out of gas. I wanted to runaway and start a new life with a new identity. My mind continued to construct thoughts and plans on ways to avoid the fury that was likely coming my way. My subconscious stayed busy at work until it was suddenly interrupted by a sharp and long "Bzzzzzzzzzzz – Bzzzzzzzzzzz – Bzzzzzzzzzzzzz." I slightly lifted my head from my arms, squinting and peering with one eye across the desk. My phone slowly came into focus to reveal the source of the commotion. The illuminated screen boldly read: "Mom." This was it; this was the impact that I had been bracing for. This was the wrath that I had been preparing to receive. She finally knew the truth and she was calling to disown me; I would soon be motherless. I would soon be on the receiving end of a bible-thumping beat down; hearing about how I was an abomination to her and god. My mind started weighing out the options; I could avoid her, or I could answer. I could get in my car and drive, never looking back, and I could go start that new life somewhere else. I could choose to disappear, or I could choose to take what was coming my way. A small bit of optimism crept into my mind; diluting some of my bleakness. "What if it went well?" I thought. There is a chance that she could prove me wrong. What if I answered that phone and she accepted me with open arms? What if she greeted me with empathy and understanding, in lieu of bigoted and homophobic rejection? "What if?" I thought to myself.

That small and slim chance was enough for me to answer the call. With one light swipe of the screen, I had my answer.

My optimism never stood a chance; it was crushed near-instantly by her rejection. Her normal loving voice was replaced by a near guttural growl that spewed her hate through the phone and into my awaiting ears. My body went into some failsafe mode of self-preservation, shielding me from her slurs as much as it possibly could. I have huge blank spots from this interaction; the tape almost appears to be erased or redacted in certain spots. My mind, yet again, trying its best to shield me from trauma. I want you to close your eyes and imagine the worst possible things that a mother could say to her son. I want you to think about the most god-awful things a mother could say to her gay son that just came out. I want you to envision these vile and despicable things; call to mind the most hurtful things you can. Now weave them with a mixture of homophobic slurs and scripture, mix that with a touch of repulsion, and add in some bits of perceived superiority. The comments ranged from, "This goes against god, you are an abomination!" to, "You can't possibly be gay, you were never molested as a child!" all the way to demands that

I, "never act on these demonic urges!" and the use of sharp stabbing slurs such as "faggot" and "homo." That is what I experienced, that was her response, and that was where things took a sharp turn for the worst. I fired back; I responded with my own outpouring of awfulness. I met pain with pain; I responded to hate with hate. I did not merely defend myself; I took things much farther. I was mad and I went in for the kill. I had thoughts of my relationship with my own daughter; imagining if someone would have treated her the way that I was just treated. It went beyond the fact that she was my mother; I was enraged by the thought of any parent treating a child of any age this way. My own paternal instincts now fueled my rage that much more. I took things much too far, and I ended up saying things that I regret. As good as it felt, anger was not the best response. At the very best, I was simply stooping to the level of my aggressor.

Sadly, my original predictions were fairly accurate. The only inaccuracy was in the fact that it was far worse than I could have ever imagined. I was disowned; I was now a living ghost to my mother. I was alive, but I was dead to her. To her, it was better to have a dead son, than a gay one. Our lives split, and they stayed that way for years. We went our separate ways and we lived our separate lives. Though we had been separated by distance, we used to speak several times a day. I would go back and visit regularly; she would spend some time out west as well. We went from being close family to nothing in an instant. We didn't talk at all; I no longer existed. This silence went on and on, and one day it just stopped. Suddenly and abruptly, years after it had started, it came to an end. We started talking again; cautiously avoiding the elephant in the room. Even though she has never asked for it, and she probably never will, I forgave my mother. To her, I'm sure she feels that she acted righteously. In her eyes, she was battling the devil himself. I would venture to say that she feels that she did nothing wrong; that her response was just and well-founded. In her mind, I was the aggressor and she was the victim. She was the victim of having a gay son; I should have never "chosen this life of sin." To this day, I know that she does not accept me, I know that she sees me as less because of who I am. She does not view me as equal or worthy; she takes my sexuality as a slight against her and her god. I still love her, and I still forgive her. I am thankful for the fact that she is back in my life. I have seen her grow and watched her start down the path of acceptance. Our relationship tends to ebb and flow; some days are good, and some are not. But there is progress being made; things are slowly getting better. Silence does not bring about betterment, that only happens through conversations.

After everything was done, after my work was complete, I was totally overcome with emotions. I was overwhelmed with happiness, sadness, anger, and everything in between. My initial wave of coming out had taken some time to complete; it had taken an unknown toll on me. All of the emotions and feelings that I had just fought through and suppressed, came flooding back. They washed over me, nearly crippling me with their strength. They poured in and filled the void in which I had long kept my secret hidden. I had just moved into my new place; I was now in the middle of a divorce and was selling my marital home. As I set on the end of my new bed, in my new bedroom, surrounded by my new home, the reality of the situation finally hit me. As I set there listening to the deafening silence that surrounded me, I had several realizations make themselves known. "I'm free… I'm out…" I said aloud. I was free; I finally had the freedom and ability to be me. There was nothing holding me back now, I had taken the first steps into my new life. I was overwhelmed with joy and happiness about my newly discovered freedom.

Just as my happiness was peaking, a dark and ominous creature entered the room; loneliness had made its presence known. In the quest to live my truth, there had been casualties. I lost more than a few friends and family members along the way. I no longer had a relationship with my mom, former friends blocked me online and avoided me at all costs, my time with my daughter was instantly cut in half, and I was 1,900 miles away from anyone who cared. Coming out is a lot like having someone close to you die; you're watching your old self die. There is the initial shock of the news, and people flood you with love and care. There are people that come out of the woodwork, most coming to your aid. It seems that everyone is there for you; a small army of support has been formed in your name. But as the days pass, people slowly trickle away. All of that love and support begins to fade into nothing. One day you awaken from your dream to realize that everyone is gone, and you are now left by yourself. You, and you alone, must now pick up the pieces of your life and move forward. It's such an empty feeling; it's like being the last one to leave a party. As I set there, staring down at the dark wooden floor of my new apartment, I could feel a slight vibration against the bed. I glanced over, revealing that I was getting a call. The number was familiar, but I did not have it saved in my phone. It was a number from back home, and it was surely a family member. After a few brief moments of hesitation, I answered it. "Hello?" I said. "Hey boy, this is your oldest brother," the words echoed back at me through the phone. I froze; I had not talked to him. In the whirlwind that had been my coming out, I had forgotten to come out to him. "I've been talking with mom and she told me," he said. I started to speak but he quickly interrupted me. "No, just let me talk first," he said. "You know that I love you, right?" he stated firmly. "Yeah," I mumbled back in agreement. "Well, I'm happy for you. Don't listen to mom, I'll set her straight, she'll figure things out on her end. You just focus on being you and being happy," he continued on to say. I was stunned; I didn't know how to respond. After my interaction with mom, I had started to assume the worst in people. I was happily proven wrong in this moment. I broke down; I was crying uncontrollably. He sought me out to give me his support and love; he defended me when no one else would. He encouraged me to march forward, and he helped to momentarily lift the shadow of loneliness from my life. He was the best ally that I never asked for. I came out to my oldest brother through my mom; what an odd turn of events. I'm sure that during the telling of my secret, it was never expected that he would support me, but he did. People will surprise you; the contradictions will surprise you.

Love, anger, dread, impatience, agony, shock, nauseating fear, happy, sad, ecstatic, and joyful, are just a few words I could throw out there to describe the emotions surrounding coming out. But one word really stands out to me; a word that makes that emotion medley soup edible. A feeling, an end-state, a declaration, all wrapped up into a single word. The feeling that I was ultimately left with after I came out was the feeling of freedom. After coming out, when every other feeling subsided, what I really felt was unadulterated freedom. After 25 years of living a life that was not fully my own, I was free to live the one I was meant to live. I don't want to sugar coat it; coming out can be hard. If you are fortunate enough to have a perfect family and a perfect group of acquaintances, you might have it a little easier than some of us. If you are surrounded by people that love you unconditionally and will accept you no matter what; things might be a little less intense. The unfortunate truth is that perfection does not exist, and most people's love is very conditional. You will not recognize friend or foe, ally, or enemy, until they are fully aware of your truth. Some will embrace you with a big warm hug, accepting you near instantly. Others will recoil with repugnance, viewing you as a disgusting and vile obscenity. Coming out is not easy; it is one of the hardest things that a person can do. The utterance of a small factual statement, one that is built up to with mountains of courage and bravery, that is coming out. The loss of family and friends, people that have declared their love and loyalty to you now gone, that is what it can mean to come out. Coming out is a gut-wrenching ordeal; one that will test you beyond your wildest dreams. You will be pushed to your emotional limits, you will face fear that you have never known, you will come face to face with people who will now hate you because of who you are, you will breakdown, you will sob, you will weep, and you will crumble. Coming out can suck! But, coming out is the most freeing and cathartic experience I have ever had. Beyond the awful that I encountered; I also discovered so much love and support. The love that I discovered while on my journey of truth telling far outweighed any hate that I found. The people who genuinely loved me revealed themselves, people stood by my side and defended me, I witnessed amazing acts of courage on my behalf, I had the blessing of people reaching out to me to thank me for my inspiration, people who would now feed off of my bravery and also come out. I discovered so much love and acceptance that I never expected to find. Coming out was an amazing experience! As much as I do not seek to sugarcoat it; I also do not wish to scare you deeper into the closet. It was one of the hardest times of my life, but it was the absolute best decision that I have ever made. Coming out was awful, coming out was amazing, coming out was everything and it was nothing, coming out was worth it.

# Relapse

There has always been something about the early morning stillness that drives me into deep contemplation. The same can be said about those nightly moments just before drifting to sleep, my mind blooms with thought. Silence waters the seeds planted by my experiences, my interactions, my fears, and my plans. A floral bouquet of possibility erupts on the dark ceiling above my bed; its colorful blossoms growing and swirling in the still darkness. Explosions of red, green, and blue, grow out of the void and come to life before my eyes. The dark green thorny vines erupt from the floor beneath my bed, slowly crawling their way up the white walls towards the blackness above. These creeping structures branching, twisting, and growing upwards to support the imagery of my thoughts above. My mind projects its predictions upon their intricate and robust framework. My imagination runs wild in the cool and still darkness of dusk and dawn; my fortune is told and vividly projected before me. It plays out my fears in stunning detail, it evokes sheer terror as it reveals to me my missteps and mistakes, and it brings into focus ideas and creations that I had not yet discovered. This bouquet of beauty and grotesqueness becomes etched upon my ceiling regularly. This arrangement of fear and hope, past and future, regret, and satisfaction, becomes the imagery of early mornings and late nights. In these rare moments of stillness, I am forced to examine my existence; silence cultivates self-reflection.

I awakened one morning to a revelation; a vivid understanding that punched me square in the mouth. Still reeling from the sudden strike, with the metallic taste of blood in my mouth, I said this realization out loud: "I am alone." For the first time that I could remember, I was totally alone. I had spent my early years surrounded by family and friends; never venturing too far from their reach. I spent my late-teens and early twenties traveling the country for work, but I would always return in due time. Upon my return, things would always pick up right where they had been left off. I then found myself thrust into marriage; solitude was unknown to me. Being alone was a completely new notion. Over the course of moving out west, becoming entangled in a marriage, and pouring every ounce of myself into my career, I had isolated myself. Coming out seemed to further this separation, temporarily drawing some people closer and pushing some out of my life all together. But my coming out party was over; all the revelers had gone home to tend to their own woes, problems, and to attend their own pity parties. The initial wave of love and support had departed months prior to this realization of loneliness; the mourners had long since gone home. I awakened this morning with a new cognizance to old, yet undiscovered facts. The morning sun greeted me with the understanding that I was alone; I did not have any real friends. Much of my family disapproved of who I was, and those that did support me were thousands of miles away. I was a fresh divorcee; I was a single father. I was surrounded by an empty and unknown home. I was disenchanted with the notion of love; the realization that I had never truly experienced it weighed heavy upon me. I found myself stuck in a career in which I was being worked to death, working non-stop for an unappreciative employer. An employer who also did not appreciate who I was personally; I found myself neck deep in a horrible work culture. I was placed in a position of covering at work. The morning greeted me with news that I was not happy; after months of change I was still not satisfied. The pain and hopelessness of hiding had swiftly been replaced by the pain and hopelessness of loneliness. My life was still not quite where I wanted it to be.

I was spiraling into an endless hole; I fell into a deep depression. How the hell could this happen? I was out! I was finally free to be my true self. I had complete unabridged freedom, and yet I was unhappy. The truth had set me free, but truth alone was not enough. Truth-telling did not grant me self-acceptance, it did not mend the mental and emotional trauma of my past, it did not make up for years of covering, and it did not magically give me some new and happy fulfilling life. I was painfully unaware of what would come after coming out; my rose-colored vision of this instant happy gay life was an illusion. I found myself in familiar, yet unwanted territory. I again found myself floating; day after day just going through the motions. I was walking the path of depression; a growing and unstoppable sadness was building in my core. A knot regrew in my stomach, a constant and nagging ache again became my companion, and there was now a growing void that I could not seem to fill. The only apparent benefit of my newfound freedom was that it allowed me to try to fill this growing hole in new and creative ways. I tried to fill it with work, but there never seemed to be enough of it to distract my mind. I tried to fill it with alcohol, but I could never quite reach the peace that I so desired. I tried to fill it with men and casual sex, but it was never enough. No matter what I tried, nothing could fill this void or alleviate my ache. I continued to float, and the void continued to grow. The more that I would attempt to fill it in, the deeper it would become.

There is just something about tearing across the California desert in the dead of night, pushing yourself and your vehicle to their absolute limits. Cool whispers of wind roll down from the surrounding mountains; they cut through the warm night air like a razor. They gently wisp through the open windows, brushing lightly against your skin. Their cool touch pulling you ever so lightly from this trancelike state of locomotion. There is just something about the desert at night; this mixture of danger and adventure is intoxicating. It pushes one faster and faster, deeper, and deeper into the mystery of the night. Small shelled out towns come and go; the glow of headlights is a near oddity. In the desert, you are alone, and you know it. I had just spent my week giving away 90 hours of my life to a dead-end job; this week was the same as thousands that came before. In the few remaining hours of my Friday, I booked a room in a California resort; I was bound for Pasadena. As quickly as I could, I ran from this miserable week. I ran for my car and I sped home; hurriedly packing a bag and making a break for it. The sun had long ago set; setting well before I found myself crossing the Arizona-California state line. With every mile I was nearing my final stop; coming closer to finding out what would come next.

There is just something about driving through the desert at night, it just puts things into perspective. I felt at home in its empty darkness; it felt eerily familiar. I momentarily caught myself drifting to thoughts of my life; that deep and nagging ache was apparently riding shotgun. All of my pent-up sadness poured over me like icy water. My fake smile, my laugh, and my jokes would not cut it here; the desert could see through my bull shit. I snapped myself from this reflection but quickly drifted back into its grasp; the desert had me locked under its spell. "What am I doing?" I thought to myself. The pain of life was finally coming down upon my head with vengeful force; the void had grown too big to hide. I could no longer hide this melancholy from others, much less myself. "I chose to live this life; I think I made the wrong choice. If you choose wrong,

choose again." I thought aloud. I was stunned by my pattern of thought, but it lacked surprise. I was not shaken by the fact that these thoughts were finding me. I was alone, I was empty, I felt like a failure, and I had again lost any hope that things would get better. A depressed and hopeless man seeks only to remedy his ailment; the cost is of no consequence. To pay with one's life, at least while thinking within these moments, seems like a bargain if it is curative. I was not shaken at the time by my thoughts; looking back they now chill me to the bone. My callousness and complete lack of fear now leave me baffled; on this night they made total sense. I was ready, I was done, and I wanted whatever mystery and adventure came next.

I eventually found myself checked into a stunning and lovely suite at a massive and historic resort. It was absolutely beautiful. I had just valeted my car and fought my way through a massive crowd of people; this joyful crowd was loudly celebrating a new union between a man and wife. I pushed my way through the celebration and towards the elevator; departing the car I went down a long and winding hall. The floorboards gave off small muffled squeaks from under the carpet as I meandered the maze of hallways searching for my room. "Nearly there!" I thought as I traced the numbers like I was searching for some hidden treasure. I used the key to open the massive double-doors; the two large doors groaned as I pushed them opened and entered the room. "This place is bigger than my apartment!" I muttered to myself as I tossed my backpack on the bed. I made my way to the gargantuan marble appointed bathroom; filling the tub as I tore off my clothes. I slid myself down into the near scalding water, closing my eyes in relaxation. For a split-second I forgot about this shadow that was following me; my demon was still fetching his bags from the car. I started to gently doze off and then suddenly awakened in a panic; my emotion was inescapable. I no longer had brief moments of sadness surrounded by large swaths of happiness and normalcy; this dull melancholy ache was my normal. These moments of escape, moments such as this one, were of the rarest nature. These small flashes of normal were my only escape from the shadow of depression that followed me.

I pushed up firmly on the cold and round edges of the old iron claw-foot tub, pushing my way up and out of the bath. I quickly toweled off in attempts to warm myself, and swiftly made my way towards my bag for a fresh change of clothes. My feet near instantly warmed as I transitioned from the cool marble of the bathroom to the plush carpet of the bedroom. I now had a few moments to explore this massive room; opening doors and cabinets to discover what treasures they held. I pushed open yet another pair of grand double-doors, revealing a beautiful stone and cement balcony. I could hear the roar of the wedding party I had just observed; they had taken the celebration outside. The loud voices and clanking of glasses and bottles only cemented my current state of loneliness. With a slight chuckle, I pushed my way back into the room, I needed to continue my adventure in exploration. I pushed on an old wooden armoire; a loud creak erupted from it as a door slowly swung open. Hiding in the darkness, I noticed a tray of snacks, a small television, and a small black refrigerator. The television crackled and popped as it awakened from its slumber; some random news channel slowly illuminated the black screen. "Peanuts, peanuts, *M&Ms*, pretzels, trail mix, and *Pringles*, I said out loud as I rummaged through the snacks. Giving up on finding quality sustenance, I made my way down towards the small humming fridge. As I pulled the door open with a slight tug, I could feel the cold air escape its small rectangular box and wrap around my still damp legs. "Jackpot!" I thought to myself as its treasures were revealed to me. The finest assortment of alcohol that one could imagine was hiding behind this series of doors. Whiskey, champagne, beer, vodka, and so much more were just waiting for someone to bring them together in a painkilling concoction. My stomach screamed out to me; I had not eaten since lunch. Its strong and vocal expression was telling me that I should eat. But nourishment could wait; everything could wait.

With clanks and rattles, a similar sounding tone to the event taking place outside, I dug out several bottles of vodka and cartons of orange juice. I fetched a cup from atop the fridge and placed it in a small opening between the television and snack tray. I twisted the small cap of the dark blue bottle of vodka; it emitted a series of small clicks as it tore through the safety seal of the bottle. "glug, glug, glug, splash," I poured its contents into the small crystal glass, and quickly followed it with a touch of orange juice. I made my way back out to the concrete and stone patio, my still bare feet absorbing the dampness from the cold concrete beneath them. 'Huh, it must have rained earlier…" I thought to myself; rain was almost peculiar now that I was accustomed to the desert life. I set down in a slightly damp patio chair, the dampness soaking into my fresh shirt. I surveyed the scene before me; the wedding party was fading but still going. I peered at the glass in my hand for a moment, I downed it in a single drink, and slammed it on the table next to me. I retrieved another small blue bottle from my pocket: "click, click, click, click, glug, glug, glug, splash." I poured another drink into the awaiting glass. I drank it down even faster than the first; I was on a mission. Drink after drink, minute after minute, I poured myself into the dark night. I poured myself even deeper into my dark thoughts, resuming the ponderings of my drive.

I found myself sitting at the foot of the plush and luxurious bed; the double-doors fully open in front of me. I was in some sweet spot of conditioned and outdoor air; this mixture of cool and warm swirling around me. It was like the mixture of fresh and saltwater coming together to form a brackish inlet. I set there gazing through the open door, seeing across the narrow patio and through the heavy concrete slats of its surrounding banister. I could see the remnants of the wedding extravaganza that had been. Small groups had broken off into more intimate conversations; their distant voices mixing with the droning on of the recycled news still echoing from my television. I set there just taking it all in; I set there and drifted deeper into the caverns of my own mind. I continued to pour and mix various drinks from the nearby refrigerator; my well of vodka had long since run dry. I set at the foot of the bed; nursing whatever poison found itself at the end of my wrist. I started to drift into sleep, my head falling and quickly snapping back into an upright position. I could not rest; the time for rest was to come later. I had much to think about and much to do before I could find slumber.

I set there in deep contemplation for what seemed like hours; carefully feeding my drunkenness to ensure I maintained an adequate level of intoxication. I needed the numbness that alcohol brought with it, I needed the courage that it could provide, and I required its assistance in tearing down the walls I had constructed around my emotions. I needed it for all that the night would bring. I again started to drift towards sleep; shaking my head to wake myself. Time seemed to flow around me so slowly; the night seemed to stand still as I contemplated what was to come next. I poured myself into all of the trauma, sadness, regret, and fear that I could pull from within me. I wanted full and unshielded exposure to all that plagued me; I wanted to look this shadow in the face. I wanted to feel everything, I needed to feel it all to make the right choice. I set there on the foot of that bed motionless; I did not cry, and I did not feel sad. I was not afraid, I was not unsure, and I was not worried. Strangely, I felt some sense of excitement. The same type of eagerness that one often feels when embarking upon some type of adventure, the exhilaration of discovery. The idea that you are on your way to explore uncharted or unknown territory; the excitement of peering behind the vail. I moved my way across the massive room and towards a beautiful mahogany desk in the corner. Upon its thick glass protective top laid several ornate pens and stationery; both imprinted with the hotel's logo and year of establishment. I set down behind the desk and pulled myself forward into it, picking up a pen and grabbing a piece of paper while in motion. I started to scribble out my feelings on the pastel pink and cream paper; I poured out my raw emotion onto that desk. I dispelled myths, I told truths, and I did my best to explain away the shock and grief that some were sure to have. I told the story of this shadow that followed me; I told the tale of this void within me. I expressed my deep love for all those that loved me; I tried to set right as much as I could. I logically and dutifully laid out my driver's license; I placed a small scrap of paper next to it listing some people to call. I explained further on another small sliver of roughly torn paper some needed basics, where my car was parked and my current employer. As odd as it might sound, I did not want my burden to become another's. I was not angry; I was not seeking some type of bitter revenge. This was my pain and mine alone; this was my weight to carry and I did not want this situation to become an encumbrance to others. This was my shadow and I was taking it with me. This was my problem to deal with; mine and mine alone.

As I pushed myself away from the desk, the wheels of the white leather office chair squealed; the heavy glass desktop shifted as I pressed against it. As I stood up, I adjusted it back to its perfect state, squaring it with the corners of the desk. I made my way back across the room, the plush and soft carpet warming the spaces between my toes. I fetched a small bottle of champagne from the refrigerator and set it on the bed. I then made my way around the room picking up empty miniature alcohol bottles and organizing as best as I could. I guess some habits die hard, I could never stand to leave a hotel room in a mess. Tonight, was not going to be any different. I tidied up and repacked my backpack, laying it in the floor next to the desk. I pulled my phone from my pocket and connected it to a small dock on the nightstand; I turned on *"Hey" by Pixies*. I pecked at the phone screen until I was convinced that the song was on repeat. I turned up the volume to a loud, but reasonable level. I did not want to be a disturbance to any of my neighbors; I did not want to be a burden. I made my way back around to the foot of the bed and resumed my seat. I retrieved the bottle of champagne next to me; I popped the cork and placed the bottle to my lips. I set there without a single thought; I felt nothing for the first time that I could remember. My head again started to drift downwards; fatigue was setting in. I closed my eyes for a few brief moments and then dutifully snapped awake. I gasped to catch my breath as I woke from this microsleep; Springing to my feet to fulfill my purpose. "It's now or never," I said out loud as the small speaker at the head of the bed continued to play repetitiously.

"Damnit!" I said as I realized that the small bottle of champagne had spilled on the bed during my brief nap. I grabbed the bottle and turned it up, chugging what little bubbly liquid remained. I made my way back across the room towards my backpack; my trancelike state was now in control. It was like I was god; looking down from the heavens watching each step made. It was like I could observe but now had no power to intervene. I watched myself partially unzipped my bag and dig through my belongings. I watched myself rummage and dig for a few moments until finally revealing what I had been searching for. Holding the bag in one hand, the other pulled up and out towards the ceiling. A long brown leather belt followed behind it; it whipped and rolled like a snake as it moved from the bag and into the room. I watched myself examine the long dark-brown piece of leather; I tugged and pulled on it to test its ability for my intended purpose. I witnessed my satisfaction with the result; I could see the pleasure on my face. I watched from my perch above; I observed myself scanning the room for something suitable. I then made my way towards the double-doors of the balcony; they groaned and hissed as I pushed and pulled on them. Satisfied with their robustness and pleased with the view, I proceeded with my sacred task. I looped the belt through itself, then standing on my tippy toes I slid the belt along the top of the door. I wedged it as far towards the door frame as I could, I needed good anchorage. I refused to be some failed suicide attempt; anything worth doing, is worth doing right. I continued to peer down upon myself in this weird out-of-body experience; I watched myself diligently move from step to step preparing the best that

I could. Leaving one of the double doors open, I pulled hard on the door with the belt wedged above. I tugged firmly until the door shut and locked into position; the belt was rigidly attached to the structure, the loop floating around 6 feet from the floor. I was out on the balcony; I wanted to do this with a view. I wanted to stare into the heavens, observing the starry night above. I watched in silence; I watched along with god. We both did nothing to stop what would happen next, neither of us cared. Apparently pleased with my work, I watched myself push that squeaky old white-leather office chair over towards my work, I pushed it through the open door and onto the concrete balcony. My 5'7" self could not quite make it up to the loop; I would require a little assistance. I watched as I meticulously placed the chair and mounted it, spinning my back towards the door. I placed the wide leather strap around my neck and positioned the buckle just under my left ear. It was already quite tight; this would indeed do. I leaned slightly forward; I could feel the pressure instantly build behind my eyes. My knees were in the chair, and I was facing the chairback. My hands firmly grasped the top of the chair, the leather squeaked as I gripped it firmly. I pushed harder against the leather strap, rolling the chair slightly forward while doing so. I began to slump downwards in an attempt to slide out of the chair; I was successful. I was now hanging from my neck, my toes just barely grazing the concrete below. My feet were dancing and moving beneath my suspended body; my natural instincts of survival were kicking in. I was near instantly transported from my birds-eye vantage point back into my body. I could hear the repetitious music begin to fade; I watched as the darkness crept into my vision. I felt the pressure growing in my head, and felt my consciousness slipping away. My vision grew darker and darker until nothing at all. The shadow embraced me; its darkness overtook me. The void swallowed me, and I was no more.

With a huge gasping inhale, I leapt from the bed! Confused and in shock I looked around the room for clues as to what had happened. The last that I could recall, I was hanging from a makeshift noose on the balcony. "Is this it? Did I do it?" I thought to myself. I must have; I watched everything happen. I watched each and every detail, I watched myself take every needed step, I witnessed my death. I had watched myself die through my own eyes; I felt myself take my last breath. I ran towards the dark mahogany desk; everything was just as I had left it. My neat and thoughtful notes still laid across the desk; my final thoughts were still scribbled on the light pink and cream paper. I made my way towards the double doors, slowly peeking around the corner. I was expecting to find a corpse; I was expecting to find myself. As my sight broke the plane of the doorway, I observed an empty balcony. In shock, I slapped and pinched myself, quickly realizing that I was very much alive. Upon further examination, I found no belt in the door and the wheeled white chair remained in its rightful place. I had set down on the foot of the soft plush bed and I had passed out; vividly dreaming the taking of my own life. I was honestly quite surprised that I was alive, it all felt so real. I broke down and I wept; I collapsed into the floor. The weight of what could have happened, the burden of what should have been, instantly turned my legs to mush. I wailed and cried; the tears flowed from me like a faucet. These were not tears of sadness, they were not tears of disappointment, they were tears of joy. I was overcome with happiness and joy; a mixture of shock and euphoria surged through my body. For the first time that I could remember, I was happy to be alive.

This vivid and morbid vision shook me; this grotesque possibility awakened me. I was pulled from the void in which I had thrown myself, I was pulled from the cold waters in which I was drowning, and my relapse again turned to revelation. I pulled myself from the hotel floor and I made my way back towards that dark mahogany desk. I examined my work; notes and items artfully arranged on the thick glass desktop. I gathered items of importance, placing pictures and my driver's license back into my wallet. I was overcome with panic as I gazed upon the note, my last will and testament laying before me. This was not meant for my eyes; this was meant for others. It sent shivers down my spine; I could not bear its sight. I tugged and pulled on the paper with rage, ripping it into hundreds of little pieces! Picking up the nearby trash bin, I swept the remains into the small metal can. With my shaking hands, I placed the receptacle back under the desk. I was on edge; my body could barely contain this boiling mixture of fear and anxiety. Have you ever experienced a really close call; have you nearly been t-boned in an intersection? Have you stared down the road to see a wrong way driver heading straight for you? Those situations, the ones in which you barely escape by the skin of your teeth, are the only things comparable to the emotions that I felt. After the screeching of tires, the blaring of horns, and the near-instant relief that comes from a narrow escape, one is left with this odd mixture of sheer terror and absolute exhilaration. This peculiar fusion of emotions that one feels after a brush with death; feelings that can only be distilled down by this type of encounter. You are happy to be alive, but you are almost happier for the experience; to have pushed so close to the thin vail that separates the living and the dead. I had stared death in the face, and I had lived to tell the tale.

I stood there in the middle of this beautiful and historic hotel room, contemplating what to do next. The room was neat and tidy; it barely appeared to be used. The only clue that gave away my stay was a neat arrangement of empty bottles near the bathroom trashcan. The bed remained made, I had merely slept atop the covers. Everything was in order; my bag was packed and sitting next to the desk. I stood there for a few moments longer, taking it all in. A feeling of panic erupted from me; I was overcome with nausea and cold sweats. I ran for the bathroom, I nearly ripped off the toilet seat as I tried to raise it. "Glug, glug, glug, splash" I expelled my gallons of alcohol from the night prior into the glossy-white ceramic bowl. My panic and anxiety from my brush with darkness got the better of me; what should have been now terrified me. Lifting myself from the cold marble floor, I made my way towards the sink. The gold antique knobs squeaked as I turned them on; I placed my mouth under the faucet to rinse the foul taste from it. I caught a glimpse of myself in the mirror; my colorless and pale skin appeared nearly translucent under the bright lights. I looked like I had seen a ghost; one was staring back at me from the mirror. I ran from the bathroom, grabbing my bag from beside the desk and heading for the door. I pushed open the large double-doors leading into the hallway; I backtracked my steps from the night prior and eventually found the valet stand. "Name, sir?" the lady behind the stand asked. "Goodman... Samuel," I replied to her. "Got it. How was your night?" she responded. I paused for a moment; I had no idea what I should say. I responded with the only logical thing that came to mind: "I survived it."

There is just something about tearing across the desert at a high rate of speed, pushing yourself and your machine to its limits. The desert, with all of its vast emptiness, gives one hope as to what could fill this void. There is just something about driving through the vacant space that brings one closer to themselves; that brings you closer to your god. You are forced into thought, you are pushed into self-examination, and you are driven to deep reflection on what has been, and what is to come. In the desert, you are alone. In the desert, you know that you are alone. I found myself on a journey that I did not expect to make, but a journey that I was happy to be taking. I was going home; I had survived. My hours alone forced me to reflect on my life; it drove me to examine this dark shadow that followed me. It pushed me to make a choice: to choose between the light or the dark. I had to choose once again between life and death. There is no choice between life and death; life always wins. If my close call had taught me anything, it was that life was always the right answer. A painful and traumatic brutal life, a life shared with an ever-present shadow, is still a life. And where there is life, there is hope. Death may contain great mystery, it can bring about an end, it can be a period on a sentence, but death lacks true hope. The taking of one's own life only masquerades as a cure. Death does quite the opposite; death is the destroyer of hope. In choosing life, I chose hope. In choosing hope, I chose the pain and suffering of life. I would rather suffer and have a chance; I would happily take sadness and potential over death and nothingness.

I won't bull shit you; I think we all appreciate a heavy dose of the truth. I will never try to sell you "5 Easy Ways to Beat Your Depression!" or "The Field Guide on How to Not Hang Yourself with a Belt!" I hope that you have figured out by now that there are no easy answers; I will put this as nicely as I can: Depression fucking blows. But suicide is never the answer to depression; it took me nearly crossing that line to learn that lesson. Death takes away any chance that you might have at redemption; death is the destroyer of prospect. I was depressed and I thought that I was alone, but I was far from alone in all actuality. I picked up my phone during my drive home and called family and friends; every person I called answered me. Every person that I spoke to expressed love and care for me; they were just mere moments away. No one knew that they were never supposed to have heard from me again; many of them are just now making that discovery. I was not alone, and I had much to live for. I had an amazing daughter, I had a pretty great family, and I had many great friends. Sure, I had a lot I needed to sort out. Life is a mess, but there is great peace in accepting life for what it is. This was my mess, and I wanted every bit of it.

I had been depressed and felt hopeless; I felt guilty and worthless. But during the remainder of my trek home, I had a great awakening. The feelings were not truly my own, they had been projected upon me. These awful and horrid things had been force fed to me for the majority of my life, I had adopted a forced ideology. Worse yet, I had believed it. In this wacky manifestation of Stockholm syndrome-ish belief, I had started to hate myself. I thought that I was an abomination, I thought that I was less than equal, I believed that I was a sinner, and inferior to my straight and normal peers. I believed it because I had been told to believe it. I believed that I was worthless, because I had been told that "people like me" were worthless; I had been told that lie for much of my life. I had heard these lies at home, at school, and at work. These mistruths had been perpetuated by family, peers, friends, and authority figures throughout my existence. During that drive through the desert, I finally let go of those lies. I finally let go of the people that crafted and perpetuated those lies. I still needed to get my head right, I needed to talk through what had been going on. I confided in select friends and talked to counselors; I found what worked for me, and I did it. I think it's important to call out this bull shit stigma that surrounds seeking help; help was exactly what I needed. Sure, I made the choice to live. I had also made the choice to let go of the lies that had been exacted upon me. But now, I had a bigger and more pressing question: How the hell do I do the rest of it?

Life is far too precious and much too short to spend it married to the shadow of depression, or to cut it even shorter by suicide. Life is too great of a gift to end it prematurely; to short-change yourself of potential. I had made the choice to live, but I still needed to get better. For me, I started to prioritize my mental health. I started to place my happiness first; I reorganized my life and really started to follow my heart. As "hippity-dippity" as that sounds, it actually worked! I stopped wasting my time on people, jobs, or things, that didn't bring me joy. It really was that simple. I hated my current job; it was soul-crushing. The culture was terrible, the office was rife with homophobia that forced me to cover, and I was being worked into the ground. I quit! I found a new job; I chose happiness above all else. I cut ties with people that did not match my energy; people that brought me down or were not accepting of who I was. You know the type, "I don't

agree with your lifestyle, but I'll still be your friend..."
Fuck those people! I let them go; I discovered that I had
no time to squander on them. I let go of a religion that
was not mine, and I let go of the fear that had me cling
to it. I let go of a congregation that used their bible as
an excuse to hate people; a religion that used this book
as a tool to justify their bigotry. I cut the cancer from
my life and I replaced it with things that I loved. I
poured myself into my happiness, and I let go of trying
to please others.

Things are now perfect in my life! I never get sad, I
never get depressed, nothing bad ever happens to me,
life is an absolute joy, I can eat whatever I please and
not get fat, my skin is always clear, I never have bad
hair days, and everything always works out in the end!
Fuck off, right? I still fight depression from time to
time, I still get sad, I still must do things that do not
bring me absolute joy, and everything does not always
work out in the end. Can you believe it? Life is not the
god damn fairy tale we were led to believe that it is. But
now, I know how to deal with those things. I know the
power of leaning on the people that I love; I know the
power in seeking help. I have learned the amazing
strength of self-acceptance, and I have discovered the

gift of taking things as they come. I have accepted my life for the messy and chaotic thing that it is, this is my mess and it brings me joy. I now choose happiness above all else; I find joy in every moment lived. I find joy in sadness and I find joy in suffering. I find joy in every moment of life. In every additional second of being that I am gifted, I choose happiness above all else.

Always remember, you are not alone.

*National Suicide Prevention Lifeline:*

1-800-273-8255

# Unobscured

How do you explain a feeling never felt? Furthermore, how do you explain the feeling of realization that feelings that you thought you had experienced were nothing more than cheap imitations? I spent my life believing that I knew what love was; that I had experienced the magic of love on many occasions. I am not talking about love for my family or friends, I'm talking about amorous love. I believed for a long time that I had known passionate, romantic, and affectionate love. I thought that I knew it well, that I had found it and lost it several times, that I knew it ups, its downs, and what it was inside, and out. But, part of my great awakening was that I did not know love at all. This grand and earth-shattering admission that I had never loved another was part of what finally pushed me from the shadows; my realization pushed me out of the closet. This life-changing moment made me realize that covering would never work, and continued hiding would only lead to a loveless life. The notion of love had completely escaped me. I spent so much of my life chasing what I was told that love was supposed to be, that I never actually found it. Finding true love is hard enough without looking for it in all the wrong places. I was chasing an image of a man and a woman, an image burned into my mind by ideals that were not my own. I was building a life to suit the thoughts of others, a life that had been predetermined for me. I was chasing something that would never work; I was pursuing people that I could never intimately love. Every romantic "I love you" that I had uttered in my life had been a lie; I knew absolutely nothing of amorous love. Believe it or not, this realization was empowering! This was an awakening in the best sense. I could now pursue real love, I could seek it in the right places, and I was no longer limited to some straight vision for my life. I was out and I was free; my entire life was just starting.

I thought straight dating was hard; my mind was blown at the difficulty of dating as a gay man. Seeking other gay men proved to be quite hard actually. Like myself, most were not very obvious. I stumbled aimlessly through this different, yet familiar process. I found myself making advances in the wrong directions and was left ultimately frustrated with the entire ordeal.

But let me say this, it was a happy frustration if there is such a thing. I was out and creating the life that I wanted; I was fortunate beyond my wildest dreams. I just had one final obstacle to figure out: Gay dating. I eventually and quite reluctantly leaned into technology; a whole new world was presented to me. I think this is a good time to level with you; a relationship was not on the menu at this time. I was out, I was single, and I was more than ready to mingle. For the first time in my life, I was openly gay. I was ready to "sow my wild oats," and that is exactly what I did. But that party faded fast, it was not what I was looking for, it was not me. That is where dating as a gay man got that much harder for me. I was tired of clubbing and casual encounters, I never really cared that much for it to begin with. I craved more; I wanted to grow something with someone. Do not take me wrong here, I was not in some big hurry. I was not out and about trying to fall in love; I actually quite enjoyed my single existence. The notion of being alone, a feeling that once pushed me into dark episodes of sadness, was now something I found to be empowering. I liked the ability to choose everything for myself; I enjoyed the selfishness that single life afforded me. I was content with life, but still desired more. Hooking up and clubbing only left me feeling empty. I needed the pursuit to be meaningful, I needed it to matter, and I needed it to take me where I wanted to go. I knew clubbing and the hookup scene wouldn't take me there; It would not aid in bringing my visions of happiness to life. I sought connection, I wanted compatibility, I wanted someone to grow with, and I wanted an actual relationship. This turned out to be surprisingly hard to find in my new world. I do not mean to perpetuate any of the stereotypes that I have often rallied against here, but love and connection is not high on the priority list for most young gay men. As I grew tired of the "scene," I just stopped participating in it. I would date but became slow to hookup, and quick to walk away if my expectations were not met. Sex was such a small part of what I really needed; I needed connection. If there wasn't some immediate sense of this sought-after connection, I would quickly walk away. I had lost any desire to play games; I had lost any patience for wasting time.

Life is funny. Fuck that! Life is simultaneously ridiculous and hilarious. After spending a couple years wandering the barren gay landscape, I now set across the table from what appeared to be a normal and handsome man. We were on our first date; we text back and forth for a week or so before we had finally mustered the courage to meet. From the instant that we had started talking, there was just something about him. There was just something in his essence that was different than anyone that I had ever met. There was a spark, a small flicker of instantaneous connection. We found ourselves in a dimly lit restaurant having drinks, and nervously creating conversation with each other. Meeting face to face only made this connection more apparent; attraction and connection met in some extraordinary and blissful showing. We set there in the dim and loud restaurant for hours; those hours felt like only a few brief moments. The sounds of glasses and plates were clinking all around us; the roar of loud conversations and laughter were just as loud. We set there drinking and talking well beyond our meal. Neither of us wanted this experience to end; we were exactly where we wanted to be.

We talked and talked; the small spark of connection grew into a flame. Our conversation continued as the restaurant neared its closing hour. As the loud roar of our surroundings shrunk into a light murmur, we finally made our way outside. Our drinks had taken effect; we used them as an excuse to linger that much longer. We walked around the expansive plaza; the cool Phoenician winter air was wrapping around us. The cool winter of the desert gave us an unneeded excuse to draw close to one another. We wandered past shops and small sitting areas filled with people; we examined the partially hung Christmas décor from shop to shop. Our conversation seemed never-ending, we talked and wandered well into the night. I didn't want to let go, I wanted it to be never-ending. I was terrified that if I walked away, I would never find this moment again. Even as we decided to call it a night, we continued to procrastinate our departure. We stood at our vehicles in a mostly empty parking lot, continuing to simply enjoy one another's company. As the police started the process of shewing away any remaining high school kids from the large outdoor mall, we finally said our goodbyes. With a light hug and a promise to do it again, one of the best nights of my life came to a close.

I was enamored with him, he seemed perfect in every way. My thoughts were flooded with him the entire drive home; he was all that I could think about. We spent the next little bit texting and continuing to stoke the flames of this new connection. We spent time together and we continued to date off and on, then suddenly, nothing. We found ourselves infatuated with each other one moment and ignoring each other the next. Neither of us quite knew what was happening at the time. I was so cautious with my affection and how I displayed it, that I held back as to not seem too interested. I purposely limited my communications; I was so afraid of coming off as, "over the top." I did not want to be perceived as crazy; I really liked him and did not want to mess this up. I was really fearful that I would scare him away, or even worse, that our feelings were not mutual. On my end, I had slowed things to a crawl, yet wondered why things were not blossoming. Looking back now, we were both doing the exact same thing. We both shared the exact same fears. We had captured lightning in a bottle, and we were both so afraid of losing it, that we were in danger of it becoming nothing at all. We continued this dance for a short while until we eventually came to our senses; we fully embraced our desires. We finally realized how much we genuinely wanted a relationship with each other, and after a while we officially started dating. Weeks turned to months; night after night he was staying at my apartment. That initial desire to not be apart remained, we never wanted to be separated. It was agonizing to feel that we had missed any opportunity to be together.

Over time, we slowly merged our lives together. Most people seem to have this big ordeal with some massively stressful conversation about this subject, but we didn't. We never had the, "Hey, should we move in together?" conversation. It just did not happen like that for us; things just seemed to flow more naturally. For us, it went more like this: "Holy shit! We're living together!" He still had his apartment and I had mine, but we really only stayed at my place. Over time, what was once my apartment, became our apartment. We just went with the flow of life; we followed our hearts and let go. We leaned into this new connection and we let life take us where it wanted.

It was a tourist filled Memorial Day weekend on the Las Vegas strip; we had just arrived after a quick 1-hour flight from Phoenix. After fighting our way through the crowded McCarran airport, a bumper to bumper Uber ride across the strip, and a long wait at check-in, we had finally arrived at our room. It was pure luck that we had made it at all; the battle through Phoenix traffic was nearly as rough and crowded. Nevertheless, the stars had aligned, and the gods had permitted our quick trip to sin city. We were here, we were together, and we were ready for an amazing weekend away. After settling and getting a bite to eat, we found ourselves back in our room. We were intertwined on the bed; we laid motionless in the silent room. We laid there just taking in the moment, we were merely enjoying each other's presence. In this still and quiet moment, a

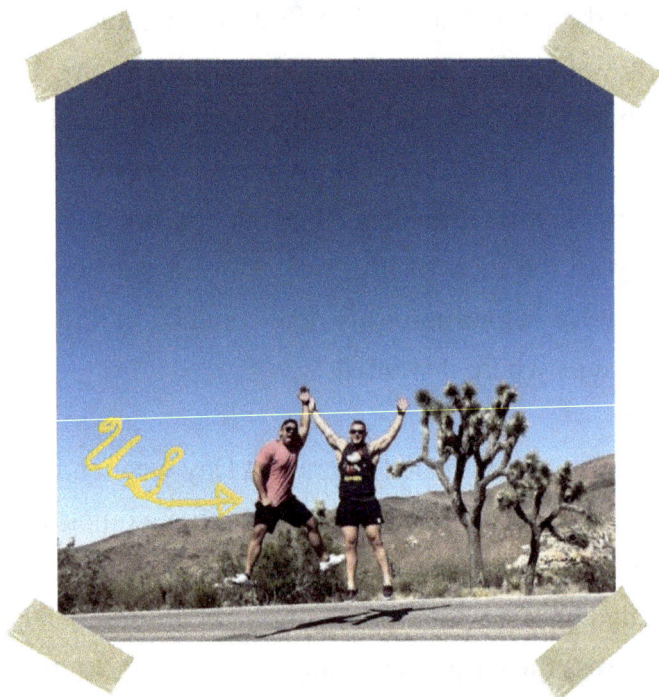

flooding of emotions wrapped around me like a tidal wave. I could feel every cell in my body come to life; chill bumps covered my skin, and I was buzzing with passion and a sense of warmth. As we laid there interlocked, I found myself staring at him. My heart raced and my breathing struggled to catch up; it was intoxicating. I was drunk without drinking a drop, I was on fire with a nervous energy. I had never felt feelings like these before. "Am I dying?" I thought to myself as this emotional tsunami continued to overpower me. "I think I'm having a stroke," I contemplated as I continued my ride on this emotional rollercoaster. I could not wrap my mind around what was happening; nothing made sense, but it felt amazing. It felt like I was holding the universe in my hands and its power was surging through every cell of my being. It felt like I had reached out and touched god; a near spiritual electricity was flowing through me. I looked at him and it all finally came together, it all instantly made sense. I stared at him in the eyes and told him what I was experiencing, I shared a new truth with him: "I love you."

After hundreds, if not thousands, of false exchanges of love, I had finally experienced the real thing. Being in the presence of true and real love only concreted the fact that I had never been in its blinding presence before. After months of on and off encounters, officially becoming a couple, and unofficially moving in together, I finally understood what that spark was the first night that we met. It was love; it was the beginnings of what I was now experiencing in full force. The mystery of love was now revealing itself to me. He stared at me in complete silence after my confession, peering back at me blankly. My electric feelings of infatuation quickly mixed with confusion and worry. "What the hell did I just do? What if he does not feel the same?" I thought as a sense of embarrassment and panic washed over me. I wanted to crawl right out of my skin, leaving it behind, and run out the door. This skinless version of me could run downstairs, catch an uber, catch a flight, and be back in Phoenix in a matter of hours. My mind set about plotting this grand escape in the microseconds of silence that followed my newly discovered awareness and confession. As I continued to gaze upon him, he appeared as if he had the wind knocked from him. He looked as if he were experiencing some sensation of asphyxiation; the breathlessness you witness when one takes a rough tumble or when someone gets punched in the gut. He appeared as if he had forgotten the need to breathe. The silence continued and everything around me slowed to a near stop; my panic quickly turned to dread as I awaited his response. What I did not realize at the time was that he was experiencing a similar, if not the same, intoxicating mixture of euphoria and panic.

We were locked in endless silence, neither of us seemed to have the ability to speak. Then suddenly, he snapped out of it and started to respond. My heart again raced; I was certain that he was about to crush my newly discovered feelings. "I love you, too," he said as he continued to stare into my eyes. From that moment on, we both knew where we stood. We knew that this was it; our worlds would become one. The panic and anxiety rushed from my body as quickly as it had found me. Its void was flooded with happiness and joy. I could feel the electricity in the air, it continued to pulse through me. I was holding pure power in my hands; I had captured lightning in a bottle.

It should be quite obvious that the discovery of real love was life changing; it was that much more life-changing discovering it so much later in life than most. The power of true love amazed me. It's power still does if I am being completely honest with you. Extra cheesy, but it's true! Love helped to heal so many wounds that I had incurred in my years prior to its discovery. Love taught me lessons that I would have never known without it, hard teachings in patience and selflessness. The power of love built our little family; it pulled us together against all odds. The power of pure and true love holds us together in a world that is often pitted against us. We are some of the lucky ones; some of the lucky few. Life seemed to direct us to one another, everything happened so naturally. Our love, our relationship, and everything about our lives together, never seemed to be forced. We managed to not only find one another, but it almost seems like we were meant to meet. We stumbled into each other's lives, we fell in love, and our little family blossomed from that love. A young man that grew up in Virginia, with no aspirations of ever going to Arizona, met a young man from California that was only in town for school, and here we are. A few seconds of delay, a moment of hurry, or just one small step pushed out of place, and none of this would be. The power of love, the power of life, it amazes me beyond words.

As I reflect on what could have been, the intricacies of life's adventure, I find myself remembering another time. Flashbacks to those moments of being hopeless and trapped; the daydreams from that season replay in my mind. The vivid visions I would manifest of the life that I so desired project in my mind's eye. It's funny looking back upon a time of such hopelessness, to now realize that all of that fantasy came true. In those moments I could have never imagined that I would be where I am now. If you would have told me that I would be happy, out, and head-over-heels in love with a man, I would have called you a liar. There is nothing that could have convinced me that all would work out in the end, but life usually does work out more than it does not. I found my way, and I am living an amazing and fulfilling life. I am finally living my life; I am walking the path that I was meant to be on. The daydreams and fantasies, the ones that I clung to for dear life, have now become my life. I have grown something out of the rubble; moving beyond my past and letting go of the mistruths that had been etched into my soul. I let go of the lies of who I was told I should be and leaned into creating who I wanted to be. In doing so, I found myself, I found happiness, I found meaning, and I discovered love.

I do not want to simply spin this as some ooey-gooey, "love will save the world, bro!" conversation, this is not that. Love was a great discovery, but it is not some end-state. Finding out what love truly meant, was a massive piece of the puzzle. But this puzzle has many bits and bobs such as acceptance, self-discovery, forgiveness, balance, and so many more pieces that range in size, shape, and importance. Getting to where I am has been a long and precarious road; it has not been an easy undertaking by any means. I have avoided bull shitting you this far, so I will not start now. This is not some "one and done" thing; this is a lifelong quest. The journey towards self-acceptance is truly never ending. Happiness is not a destination; it is found in the pursuit. Love is not the end all-be all, it is the glue that binds it all together, and it must be maintained. Love, though a sizeable piece of my puzzle, is still just a piece of the puzzle. Without all the other needed parts, love would never be sustainable. Discovering the feelings of true love helped me on my journey of self-acceptance, it was a catalyst. Feeling love in its purest form validated everything, it proved me right. All that I had felt, all that I had experienced, everything that I knew about myself, was authentic and genuine. Feeling the difference between counterfeit and legitimate love allowed me to lean into my real self.

The act of self-acceptance is an ongoing task; a fight against a world in which different is normally viewed as bad. The practice of self-care and love must be never ending, an unwavering piece of life. All of this is a constant pursuit; a task in which I have failed at many times and will continue to fail at miserably. But to truly describe where I am now, I would have to say that I am accepting. I accept that I will fail at all of that and much more, and I will fail at life with frequency. I will clumsily muddle my way through this sticky and chaotic life; I will fail repeatedly, and it will all be just fine. I have leaned into the fact that perfection is an illusion; life is chaos. The difference nowadays is that I am ok with that notion. I have accepted that life will be amazing, that it will suck, that it will throw me curveballs, that it will be chocked full of tragedy and sadness, that I will encounter unaccepting and bigoted ass holes, that I will find amazing and loving people, and that it will be overflowing with happiness and joy. I accept that my version of life is mine, and mine alone. I accept those things now because I finally accept myself.

To get better, I had to choose to get better. I had to really sort out what were my views and beliefs, and what had been placed upon me by others. I had to really pour a significant amount of time into untangling my life and the beliefs that impacted my views about myself, my sexuality, and ultimately who I was. As I poured through all of these things, I found that the vast majority of impactors on my self-acceptance were not of my own belief system; I still clung to the bits and pieces of hate that I had been taught throughout my life. I still held the beliefs of others deep in my heart. Letting go and moving on from those things was the first step; it was a massive step forward in my life. Letting go of the opinions that others had instilled in me made room for my own. I could now really build who I was and accept myself. I now had room for the growth of love, I had space for my own beliefs, I could fit in anything that I wanted. I could cut out this and that; I could declutter my soul! Letting go and cutting the fat caused more personal growth than I can even begin to describe; it was addition by subtraction. In the void that I had created by slicing and dicing out what was not mine, I grew and cultivated myself. I grew an accurate and better version of myself; an unobscured edition of me.

I want to say this, I want to scream this loudly to you, I want to make sure that it comes across clearly: I am thankful for all of it. I am so thankful for all that I have experienced in life; I accept it all for the grandiose lesson that it is. Pain, pressure, sacrifice, struggle, depression, happiness, and all things life, have made me the person that I am. This journey, with all of its chaotic twists and turns, has led me to this exact place in time and space. Do I wish that things might have been a touch easier? Can I look back with a yearning that people were more accepting and less hateful? Do I wish that growing up gay could have been easier? Of course! But now, rather than looking backwards with those thoughts, I look forward with those thoughts. I look forward with an optimistic view of making things better, of making the world a better place. I am thankful for all that I have experienced in this complex and chaotic

existence, but I hope to make things a little easier for others. I am grateful for what has been and what is yet to come; I accept life in all of its beautiful disorder. Though acceptance does not necessarily mean agreement; I still hope to make things better for all of us. I am thankful for this tumultuous life; life is an opportunity and it is a gift. This existence has given me an amazing daughter, an incredible partner, and a story to tell. A story of conquering the odds and fulfilling one's destiny; a tale of becoming true to yourself and pulling yourself out of darkness.

My story is not special, and it is not all that unique. So many people, especially those within the queer community, face a similar experience. Many have it much, much worse than I have ever encountered. I hope that there can be some lessons gleaned from my experiences and the telling of my story. More so, I hope that through my vulnerability, I encourage others to perform acts of courageous vulnerability. The telling of one's own unabridged truth is about as vulnerable and courageous as it gets; I hope to inspire more to share what they have gone through. I hope to inspire and encourage storytelling; the telling of stories is the oldest form of education. The sharing of our experiences shines a light upon the issues that are faced by the LGBTQ+ community. As each story is told a domino-effect begins to take place; each act of vulnerability leading to another, and another. I hope for this to be a catalyst for that ripple effect; acts that lead to learning and understanding by those that would normally not hear the message. Storytelling can change the world; the act of storytelling can make the world a better place.

If there is one thing that I can leave you with, it is this. Scream your truth from the roof tops! Live a life of your choosing; be unapologetically you first and always. Gay, straight, or anything in between, be true to yourself first, then share your story. Someone out there needs it; someone needs to hear from you. Tell your story, share your life with those around you, and be vulnerable. We need more storytellers, we need more vulnerable people in this world, and we need more truthtellers. I promised myself long ago to be all three; I promised that I will fight to make things better. I will demand better. I will stand up for better. I will scream and yell for better. I will remain visible, vigilant, and tell my story. I ask this of you as well; we share the responsibility to make things better. Betterment is a group exercise, and together we can make the world a better place.

.

www.ingramcontent.com/pod-product-compliance
Lightning Source LLC
Chambersburg PA
CBHW071740270326
41928CB00013B/2749